To Mike

from [illegible]

from a [illegible] shooter to
a [illegible] barrel.
or vice versa.!!

Best wishes

Nov. '83

A LINE ON SALMON

By the same Author

THE GREAT SALMON RIVERS OF SCOTLAND

A SALMON FISHER'S ODYSSEY

John Ashley-Cooper

A LINE ON SALMON

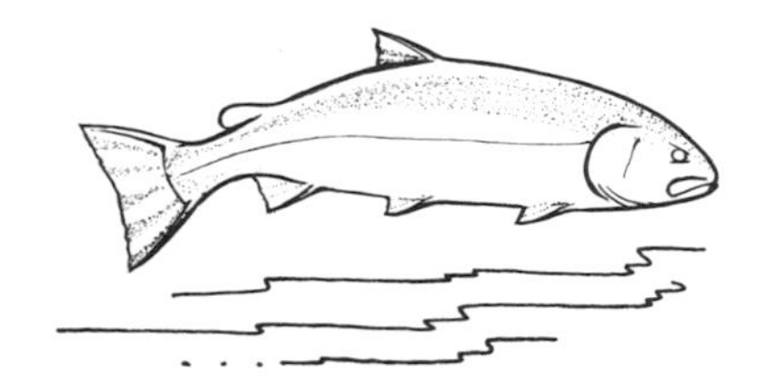

H. F. & G. WITHERBY LTD

First published in 1983 by
H. F. & G. WITHERBY LTD
32 Aylesbury Street, Clerkenwell
Green, London, EC1R 0ET

ISBN 0 85493 143 0

Filmset in Monophoto 12pt Apollo
and printed in Great Britain by
BAS Printers Ltd
Over Wallop, Hampshire

Introduction

One of the chief merits of salmon fishing is that it provides plenty of both need and opportunity for thought. Mr. W. L. Calderwood, who in the early years of this century was Inspector of Salmon Fisheries for Scotland, wrote:

'So it seems that our front line angler calls up from the depths of his hunting past some special qualities. He also lives in close touch with nature—in his case with his sport; *he is always thinking about it,* always practising it. He is not only acquiring more and more skill, he is getting further into the heart of the matter. His spirit becomes more and more attuned to the subtleties of the game. He has acquired a flair for catching fish'. These are telling words.

Admittedly 'catching fish', as has often been pointed out, is by no means the be-all and end-all of angling. Is it not rather the surmounting of a difficult problem, coupled with delightful surroundings and pleasant company which is the over-riding attraction? Does not the appreciation of and the attempt to understand all that lives in or around the river also count for a great deal? Likewise the self-control which is necessary if the fisherman is to arrive at even a moderate level of skill, and the ability to submerge individual aspirations, intense though they may be, in the camaraderie of angling friends and companions.

Surely the approach to all this cannot be severed from

a long process of thought and reflection. In the simpler words of a bygone undisputed authority, angling is 'the contemplative man's recreation'. Indeed unless the salmon angler when in action can concentrate wholly and entirely on the process of his fishing and all that goes with it to the exclusion of all outside matters, he is unlikely to achieve any great success. In this way fishing is or should be an all-absorbing process, the effects of which are akin to a temporary brain-washing. I remember once hearing an apt description of one of my fishing friends, 'Oh yes! A. is a great fisherman—I've known him sit down on the bank from time to time and really think!'. Just how many of us are prepared to forego even a few minutes of valuable fishing time to do exactly this, and whether on the river or off it to devote time to painstaking and constructive thought about fishing and all that goes with it? It is this attribute which I have in mind, and am trying to depict, though in a doubtless inadequate way. I remember the remark of my erstwhile Itchen waterkeeper with reference to pike and the perpetual war against them: 'He'm cunning, so us must be cunning too'. Quite right! and it is a similar attitude that should be adopted by the successful salmon angler instead of blindly following in the already well-trodden steps of tradition leading, it may well be, to frustration and disappointment. Only with the exercise of such thought, coupled with the benefit of extensive experience, can any of us hope to sip at the heady draught of assured confidence and to merit the exalted title of 'master fisherman'.

This book is merely an attempt to arouse amongst my fellow fishermen, such of them as are kind enough to read it, a spirit of enquiry, and to give them reason to think more closely about the many varied aspects of their sport,

thus obtaining from it a fuller measure of satisfaction. It consists of a series of essays on many different subjects, though all to do with fishing, to be picked up at any moment and delved into at random. If it is easier to write this way, perhaps it may be easier also to read. In any case, if any of the following chapters are of interest or entertainment to my readers and give them food for further thought, I shall have succeeded in my object.

John Ashley-Cooper
Wimborne St. Giles
1983

Contents

IV

SHOOTING A LINE

Colour Photographs

Author's Acknowledgements

It is with great pleasure that I acknowledge the help I have received in preparing this book from my publisher, Mr. Antony Witherby, who has at all times provided encouragement and valuable advice. Mr. T. Andrews has ably fulfilled the role of illustrator, and the delightful drawings herein are all the products of his skill.

For their help in providing essential information for the chapter on dry-fly fishing for salmon, about which I myself know so little, my grateful thanks go to Mr. M. Lunn, to Dr. Wilfred Carter of the International Atlantic Salmon Foundation of New Brunswick, to Mr. H. G. Wellington of New York, to Colonel Henry A. Siegel of the Angler's and Shooter's Bookshelf of Goshen, Connecticut, to Mr. Shirley E. Woods of Ottawa and to Mr. Lee Wulff and his book *The Atlantic Salmon*. I am greatly in their debt.

Finally I would like to thank my many friends for their kindness and hospitality, and particularly for their invitations to fish on their waters, as a result of which so much of the material for this book has been acquired. In particular I would like to thank Major Sir David Wills for so many delightful opportunities of fishing the splendid Knockando water on the Spey over a long period of years; but my grateful thanks go to all of them.

I

THE FISH

1

Conundrums and Questions

The salmon has always been a mysterious fish; and although of recent years much has been discovered about his habits, migrations and life-cycle, there is fortunately still a good deal about him that we do not know. I say 'fortunately', as the more that is known, particularly of his sea movements and habitats, the more he is laid open to exploitation by unscrupulous commercial fishermen. And even when he has returned to fresh water and can be kept under close observation there are still some inexplicable aspects of his behaviour.

It is this latter period in the salmon's life cycle which is of closest interest to anglers, and the following chapter is an attempt to arouse the reader's interest by some random but pertinent queries about the salmon, his habits and behaviour. Some of these queries, in our present state of knowledge, are unanswerable, though they may give food for thought. To others a suggested answer is given which may or may not be correct, but again may serve to arouse thought or discussion.

Why, if spring salmon are not going to spawn before October or November, do many of them enter fresh water as early as December, January, and February?

They then remain in the river for some nine or ten months, without feeding, before fulfilling their reproductive role which so far as we know is the only reason why they leave the sea.

This seems a curious mis-provision of Nature. One would have thought that the entry into the river of the autumn fish, which arrive fresh run in September, October, or November, was much better timed. The spawn of such fish is well-developed, and they are going to spawn after only a short interval. If you cut open a spring fish, on the other hand, you will find the spawn by contrast developed only to herring-roe size, or the milt hardly apparent at all. Such a long sojourn in fresh water does seem illogical if not inexplicable. Surely an extra five or six months of luscious sea feed would provide a far better preparation for the exertions of spawning, rather than a nine month fast?

The only possible explanation might lie in the fact that spring fish almost invariably spawn far up in the headwaters of their chosen river and it takes time to reach them. Summer and autumn fish, although some do penetrate far upstream, are apt to spawn indiscriminately over the whole river system, often in the middle or lower reaches down to within a mile or two of tidal water, wherever there is suitable gravel. The behaviour of the spring fish may thus perhaps be in accordance with Nature's demand to have the spawning process spread as widely as possible to ensure against some natural disaster such as excessive floods or frost ruining the reproduction of fish in any one particular area. Consider for instance what happens in a river like the Tweed which has entirely separate spring and autumn runs. The early spring fish by the time their spawning season in October arrives are far up in the headwaters of Ettrick, Yarrow, or Tweed near Peebles, at least sixty miles up-river. It is rare for a stale spring fish to be caught in autumn anywhere below Ettrick mouth, i.e. in the middle or lower river. On the other hand, although fresh run autumn fish are to be found in due course as high up as Peebles or Selkirk, some of them spawn in the main river or tributaries as far down as the Coldstream area, and many in the middle reaches.

I know this does not amount to a convincing explanation of the high-upstream spawning habits of spring fish, as why for that matter could not more autumn fish show enough energy to permeate right to the headwaters? There is usually plenty of water when they make their entry, and nothing apparently to stop them doing so.

On the other hand can anyone provide a better explanation of the spring fish's so pronouncedly early entry? A possible explanation which has been put forward to account for this early entry is that the spring fish have reached a stage in their sea life where they are replete with food and for the time being are surfeited. They therefore seek their parent river, where they enjoyed their early life, primarily as a resting place and shelter from their many salt water enemies. Only later, after several months in the river, does the spawning urge develop. This may perhaps be a part truth, but it is not wholly convincing. Why, if it were the case, do we not have salmon entering rivers and dropping back to the sea without spawning for the time being?

In this connection one is reminded of the Tweed netsmen's theory of 'Westerners', i.e. spring fish which they describe as being caught in their nets when dropping back from river to sea without spawning. Whether this is a fair assumption of fact or not is however open to doubt. Such a movement of fish does not seem to occur in other rivers, except after outsized spates, and a preponderance of Tweed springers in any case most certainly does spawn.

How does a salmon navigate thousands of miles back to his own river, which he left as a smolt some two years earlier, and after migrating perhaps as far as the west coast of Greenland?

The migratory instinct is indeed a remarkable one. We are told that swallows and house martins return to nest under the same eaves as they themselves were reared, having migrated as far as the Sudan in the meantime. Henry Douglas-Home in his delightful book *The Birdman* recounts how a tame grouse at Cawdor in Scotland was packed in a hamper and transported south to Henley-on-Thames. There this bird after a day or two was missing from its pen, and within a few days had reappeared in its old haunts at Cawdor having completed the 500 mile return journey on its own initiative.

But such exploits pale beside the migratory achievements of the salmon. That the survivors of the smolt migration do return as adult grilse or salmon to their parent river, except for a very small proportion which lose their bearings and reappear elsewhere, is now an established fact. It has been made clear by tagging experiments in Scotland, on the North Esk and elsewhere. Tagging has also shown that a considerable number of our British two sea-winter fish travel as far as the Davis Strait off the west coast of Greenland. This is a distance (crow flight) of 3000 miles (plus), and as the fish swims a great deal further. As a matter of interest an average of 12 miles per day would be the minimum required for a fish to cover this distance, and when he is really on the move an adult fish would presumably swim at far greater speed. The amazing fact remains that a tiny smolt of five or six inches length, provided he survives, develops enough homing insinct after one, two, three, or four years in the ocean to find his own way back, not only to his native river, but probably to the same area in it where he himself was bred.

One has read various theories as to the way in which salmon navigate, e.g. by the sun, the stars, the ocean currents, and eventually the taste or smell of the water from their parent river. Except for the last, none of these are wholly convincing. And why do some of our salmon travel as far afield as the Davis Strait when others obviously make for different feeding grounds? And where are the sea feeding grounds of our grilse? Presumably they are closer at hand, as these fish only remain for one year in the sea.

It is still all largely a mystery, as is everything to do with the migratory instinct, and long may it remain so! One need hardly point out, for example, that before the salmon feeding grounds off Greenland and off the Faroes were discovered there were many more fish off our coasts and in our rivers.

The angler, whose observation of the salmon is confined largely to its river life, can offer little or no helpful evidence on the subject of its wider migration. In my own case however two small points have struck me as being of possible side-interest, as follows:

For many years I fished for two or three weeks every season in Iceland and caught and saw many salmon and grilse on the north and west coast of that island. These were Atlantic salmon of the same species as our own, with exactly the same appearance except for two minor differences. One was that fresh run Icelandic salmon always seemed to cut paler on the table than fresh run British fish. Their flesh lacked that deep rosy pink which is such an outstanding characteristic of our fish. And the second was that the teeth of fresh Icelandic salmon were more numerous and pronounced than those of our fish. Fresh Icelandic fish had long and sharp teeth, like those of well mended kelts. It seemed that these two facts gave some side-indication on the migratory habits of both British and Icelandic fish. The former seemed to have different feeding grounds more liberally endowed with crustaceans or some form of food which produced that rich rosy-coloured flesh. Also it appeared that Icelandic salmon when they entered fresh water were closer to their feeding grounds than British salmon, in that there had not yet been time after the cessation of regular feeding for their teeth to disappear or be absorbed. This supposition was also supported by the greater keenness with which Icelandic salmon would take. They seemed to have barely lost their feeding habit, and would take more voraciously than their British counterparts.

Why do salmon jump so frequently in rivers, and so often start and stop jumping at the same time?

The name 'salmon' is by origin a Latin word derived from 'salmo' the leaper (cp. Latin salire—to leap). Salmon jump more frequently than any other fresh water fish; sea trout and brown trout are jumpers too, but not to the same extent.

The Roman legionary when he reached the Atlantic rivers of north Spain, trans-Alpine Gaul, and Britain must have regarded with interest the abundant shoals of leaping salmon, far more numerous than in modern times, to be found in so many places.

Salmon as we all know will jump to amazing heights in order to overcome obstacles to their passage upstream.

As Izaac Walton delightfully quotes from Michael Drayton's Polyolbion:

'Here, when the labouring fish does at the foot arrive,
And finds that by his strength he does but vainly strive,
His tail takes in his mouth and bending like a bow,
That's to full compass drawn, aloft himself doth throw;
And if at first he fail, his second summersault
He instantly essays; and from his nimble ring,
Still yerking, never leaves until himself he fling
Above the opposing stream . . .'

A fair picture; except for the misconception of the tail in the mouth. It is always fascinating to stand by a fall in time of spate and watch the astonishing exertions of the fish in their efforts to surmount the obstruction.

But it is not this type of jump which is of most interest to the angler. It is rather the fish that jumps for apparently no reason in a likely lie which arouses his interest and his hopes. When there are a number of fish in a pool it is curious how they will start jumping in numbers at a given moment. To start with perhaps none will jump, then an odd fish here and there, and then in a matter of minutes they will be jumping all over the pool, with three or four fish in the air at a time. After a limited period however it may seem as though their energy for the time being is exhausted, and they will return to their lies to remain apparently dormant, until the next bout of activity. Why do they do this? Is it simply because they enjoy jumping, or are there other additional reasons, such as sea lice irritating them, or the pain from raw patches induced by U.D.N. becoming intolerable? Perhaps such causes are all contributory.

From time to time, of course, in a river such as the Spey in springtime, when fish are much on the move, the whole pool for perhaps ten minutes will become alive with jumping fish, and then go dormant. This is not necessarily due to any unwonted burst of activity on the part of the fish, but simply because a large shoal of running fish, perhaps 100 or 200 of them has passed through the pool, jumping as it goes. Again and again one has seen this happen. But in contrast when a pool has been well stocked with resting fish there are often spasmodic bursts of activity which have very much the same appearance. One notices certain rules which seem to govern fish jumping. For instance they seldom jump in the dark, and seldom when the air becomes markedly colder than the water. They jump more frequently when the water is warm than when it is cold, except when it becomes very warm, say to 68°F or warmer, when all activity is likely to cease (unless there are some lively new-run fish around). They seem to jump more frequently when present in numbers, and the solitary fish seldom shows. Is it that one or two lively fish in a pool will stir their companions up to a burst of activity? Or is there possibly some other cause—for instance does a change in barometric pressure induce them to jump in order to release air from their swim bladder?

We simply do not know the answer to these conundrums, nor do we know why kelts also are addicted to jumping, in spite of their emaciated condition. Nevertheless fishermen should be grateful for this brand of activity. Many an energetic salmon has lost his life by advertisement of his presence through a vigorous jump. It has sometimes been said that jumping fish do not take. I would not agree with this. Often they do not, it is true, but often also they do. There is no hard and fast rule here, and the sight of fish jumping in numbers in the water he is about to fish is surely a welcome encouragement to the angler's morale.

It goes without saying that the fisherman should be able to distinguish with fair certainty between the jump of a running fish and a resting one. This is not always easy, and occasionally impossible; see drawings on pages 52/3. Needless to say, so far as fishing over him is concerned, the running fish should normally be ignored. It is also important in springtime to be able to distinguish between the jump of a fresh fish and a kelt. One wants to waste no time fishing over kelts. In the spring of 1982 I was told that a certain beat on the Tay, which we were due to fish the following week, was full of fish jumping everywhere. So it was, as we found out when we got there, but 99% of these fish unfortunately were kelts. My informant did not know the difference between the jump of fresh fish and kelts, so once again our hopes were thwarted!

Incidentally salmon and grilse also jump frequently in the sea, as any coastal netsman will tell you. And many of them as a result lose their lives to 'splash netting'.

Perhaps the most intriguing jump of all would be that of a salmon leaping out of the water to seize one's fly in the air as it dropped towards the water at the end of the forward cast. What a sight that would be! I believe it is on record as having occurred, though neither any of my friends, so far as I know, has experienced it, nor have I myself. I have twice had it happen in Iceland, however, that a salmon was so excited at the appearance of my fly that he did a complete porpoise jump out of the water to seize it on his re-entry through the surface. That was certainly a sight worth seeing, and in both cases it resulted in a fish firmly hooked and later beached.

But we are still left without any certain explanation as to why the salmon jumps in the manner and to the extent which he does. It is a riddle to which only increased scientific knowledge may in the future provide the true answer.

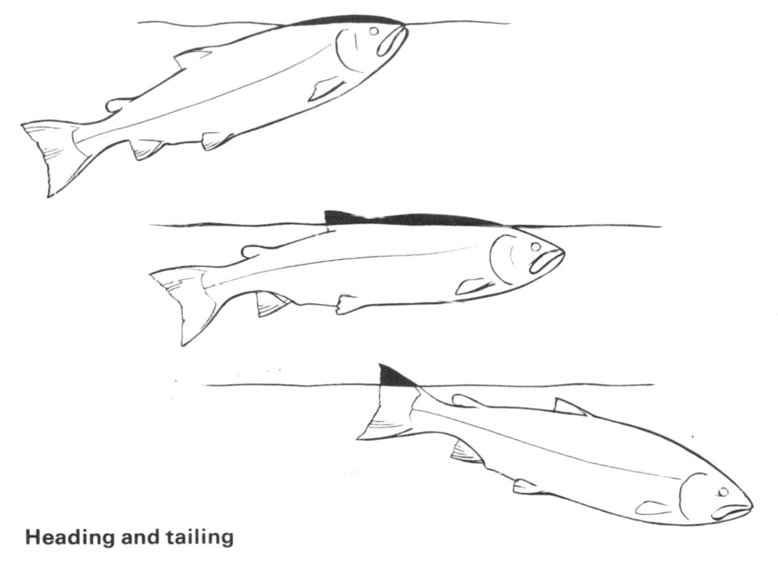

Heading and tailing

Why if a sea-trout will take the artificial fly in pitch darkness will a salmon not do so?

This I believe to be a true statement of fact, though the practice of fishing for salmon in pitch darkness is not likely to be generally popular! Perhaps it would be more so, if greater success attended it. We are told that the sea-trout in summer, as long as the water is low, take best between twilight and early dawn, particularly during the hours of black darkness. And it is not necessary at such times to use an outsized fly—they appear to see and take an ordinary fly of size 8, 9 or 10 perfectly well. Why then do salmon not follow suit? Their eyesight is presumably no less keen than that of sea-trout. In summer they will take in the twilight both of late evening and early dawn; but very seldom when all the light is gone. In spring or autumn it would be a waste of time fishing for them during the hours of darkness. With the coming of dusk, as the air begins to cool, they are apt to shut up shop and not to take until the next morning's risen sun has apread light, warmth, and vitality into the river and its surroundings. I must admit that I do not know the answer to this question. Can any of my readers suggest one? Undoubtedly it is just as well that salmon do *not* take all round the clock, as this affords them a certain measure of well-needed protection in these days of intensive fishing.

Why when a salmon will readily take a still prawn or shrimp will a sea-trout never do so? The salmon may be in the guise of a 4lb. grilse, and the sea-trout weigh 12 or 14lb. but this makes no difference.

This is a curious actuality, but none the less true. It is inexplicable in our present state of knowledge, but there must be some well-founded reason for it. Possibly the salmon's wide sea-range carries him where red ocean crustaceans of one sort or another form a substantial part of his diet, and to where sea-trout never penetrate; but would grilse range that far? They are just as keen on prawns and shrimps as their larger brethren.

It may be of little significance from the salmon fisher's point of view that sea-trout eschew prawns, nevertheless it arouses one's curiosity. Incidentally they will take spinning prawns or shrimps but that is another matter. And to those of my readers who are dedicated fly fishermen

the whole subject is no doubt repugnant.
My apologies to them!

Why do big fish not enter small rivers?

This seems a simple question and the answer an obvious one, that there just isn't room for them—but there is a bit more to it than that. Just consider for a moment a small river of the west coast type, where a fish of 15lb. is an outsized one. Its parr smolt at two, or more likely three years. They then have the same chances of sea feeding as any other smolt from any other river, large or small. We are told that the size of an adult salmon depends chiefly on how many years it spends in the sea, feeding there, before it returns to its parent river to spawn; and that it is to their parent river which the vast majority of adult fish do in due course return. It also depends to some extent on the quality and quantity of sea food which they find, i.e. returning adult fish of the same generation can differ considerably in weight. This is all quite acceptable, and has been made clear through scale reading and tagging.

In big rivers such as the Tay, Spey or Wye we find grilse (one sea-winter fish), small salmon (two sea-winter fish), and large salmon, if they have not been killed on long-lines or by drift nets (three or even four sea-winter fish). But in small rivers this last class of fish is rarely if ever found, and the stock restricted to two sea-winter fish and grilse. Why should this be so? The smolts of that river have just as good a chance in the sea as smolts from other big rivers, and why too should some of them not delay their return for three winters at least? They would then be somewhere between 16 and 35lb. in weight, if not heavier. If they were frightened owing to their large size to enter a small spate river in summer, they could wait until the autumn floods gave them greater protection.

But in fact this does not happen; and in small rivers, except on very rare occasions, we find a small race of fish. A big fish in a small river especially in time of attenuated summer flow is obviously out of place, and would be unlikely for several reasons to survive for long. So the only answer I can suggest to the original question is that Nature in such rivers provides a stock of fish which do not stay for more than two winters in the sea—though how she does this, when allowing some fish from bigger rivers to spend three or even four winters there, before returning to spawn, is difficult to understand.

It seems that with salmon, as with so many other creatures, it is all basically due to the influence of heredity—that grilse breed grilse, two sea-winter fish their like, also three and four sea-winter fish their like. The only other possible solution might be that the bigger fish are afraid to enter their small parent river, and seek a larger river elsewhere. But this seems unlikely, except perhaps in rare instances, as it is against the salmon's proven migratory procedure. Apart from this there would seem to be no other possible answer.

The theory has also been put forward that big adult salmon result from big one or two year smolts, of the sort that are found in the Wye, Test, Avon, Frome and other similar rivers where the food for parr is abundant. Also that badly fed parr in small rivers where food is lacking produce small smolts and eventually small adult fish. This sounds a reasonable hypothesis, until one considers the Norwegian salmon, which on average are the biggest of all, yet the river-feed for parr, owing to the severe climate, is so sparse that they often smolt only after four years, or sometimes even five. This would seem to invalidate this whole theory. Indeed we still have a lot to learn about salmon and their way of life.

Why do kelts in Britain, when they have finished spawning, not return as soon as possible to the sea?

This again is a curious phenomenon, for which there is no apparent accounting.

One would have thought that such kelts as survive the exertions of spawning would be only too ready as soon as possible to drop back to salt water, and recoup their vitality, thanks to the rich sea-food which awaits their descent. Instead of which, in spite of their long pre-spawning fast, and with the object of their river ascent fulfilled, they are apt to linger in fresh water, still without regular feeding, for months rather than weeks, even into April and May.

One could understand this behaviour if the water level was apt to be so low that any fish movement downstream was hazardous. Occasionally it is true that some rivers remain icebound at low summer level during January, February and March, which could effectively check the downstream passage of kelts. But on the contrary there are more often floods at that time of year, and still many of the kelts do not go. Kelt mortality as a result must be abundant. In fact, it is the rise in water temperature in April or early May which seems to be the deciding factor in inducing kelts finally to leave the river, rather than any rise in the water level. It is all most curious. It would be interesting to know what happens in other Atlantic salmon countries. In Iceland for example all kelts that are able to do so wisely leave fresh water by November, immediately after completing their spawning. Otherwise they would be caught by the winter freeze up, and almost certainly perish. It would be interesting to hear what happens to the Canadian and Norwegian kelts, where the winter is as cold or colder, and when they time their descent.

Why do stale cock fish become red, and stale hen fish black after sojourn in fresh water?

There could be no greater contrast between the thrilling silver sheen of the fresh-run salmon or grilse, and its drab appearance, degenerating eventually to nothing short of hideousness, after a lengthening stay in fresh water.

The ugliness of the male fish becomes particularly apparent. His sides become a dirty red and his belly grey or yellowy. The female fish assumes a general colour of rusty black with a grey belly. No doubt this change is due to the long fast which these fish have undertaken, coupled with a change in their anatomical make-up, and the fact that such nutriment as is available in their body has been largely absorbed into the ripe milt or ova.

That such fish should be thin is readily understandable, but why do they undergo such a remarkable change in colour? Most creatures in bird or animal life adopt their most handsome array at breeding time, in complete contrast to the salmon. One can only assume that Nature provides them with this sombre exterior as a protective camouflage.

How conspicuously the white sheen of the flanks of a fresh-run fish shows up while he is being played! and how easy it is at any time to spot the presence of fresh fish in clear water when they 'flash', i.e. turn on their side momentarily, when they are restless in their lie. But as they begin to adopt their 'spawning livery', i.e. their fresh water garb, they become by stages far less noticeable.

No doubt in the sea silver flanks, white belly, and blue-black back provide good camouflage. Many fish that swim to no great depth in the sea adopt a similar colour scheme. When seen from beneath against the background of the sky or the broken surface the silver and white is presumably as unnoticeable as any colour can be. In the river too, kelts, as their river life approaches its end, regain their original silver and white protective colouring in preparation for their return to the sea. But such colouring would offer poor protection at any time in a river's shallow pools, and seen against a sombre rocky or gravelly bottom. On shallow redds in the spawning season it would be worse.

Instead Nature in her wisdom does her best to put the account straight; and so as the season passes on we find Scrope's 'muckle kippers' or 'mickle rowaners' in their unpleasing yet protective inconspicuousness. Like soldiers on active service in their khaki or camouflaged uniform, their goal is to harmonize their appearance with the prevailing hues of the background.

If salmon do not feed in fresh water, why do they take at all, and why when a pool is well stocked with fish will only perhaps one or two of them take and the others all stay aloof?

That salmon do not feed in fresh water is now beyond dispute, although it has only recently been generally accepted. The fact that their stomach and gut, when they are caught in a river is invariably empty is conclusive proof of this. One has to look no further, even though at times they are to be seen rising at natural flies such as Mayfly or March Brown. They will also take worms, which may be found in their mouth or gullet. But such 'food' is eventually expelled from their mouth, so such authorities as P. D. Malloch assure us, and is neither digested nor absorbed into their system so as to form nutriment. Consider by comparison that other prominent member of the Salmo genus, the brown trout. He is a fish which we know from observations is a voracious river feeder. When caught and opened up his stomach and gut is often stuffed with food, in complete contrast to that of the abstemious salmon. Also if salmon fed (in the normal acceptance of the term) in fresh water, every parr, brown trout, and herling would be exterminated. Pools would be aboil with salmon at frequent intervals searching for their prey, which they patently are not. There is no need to pursue this matter further.

Why then do salmon take the anglers' lure, whether fly or bait? This is a well-worn anomaly, but perhaps still of sufficient interest to merit consideration. There could be more than one answer.

When salmon arrive in a river fresh from the sea, they have only recently left their sea feeding grounds, where they have partaken greedily over a long period of any food available. Although the urge to breed has now subordinated the urge to feed, and the salmon's sharp sea-feeding teeth have been largely lost, it seems likely that the fish's feeding instinct or the predatory instinct, in spite of his state of physical repletion, has not been totally obliterated. The change may come gradually rather than instantaneously; indeed one would expect this. For example, fish caught in sea nets along the coast are often found to contain herring. It seems natural therefore that fish should retain sufficient of the sea feeding urge to take more keenly in a river when they are *still fresh run*, as they undoubtedly do; and they are more inclined to take flies or baits of larger size, approximating more closely, one might imagine, to their recent sea food.

After they have been in the river for a fair period of time, they become noticeably less keen to take. This may well be due to a gradual falling off in their sea feeding memory or habit (however you like to phrase it), and in their physical condition, owing to their prolonged fast, making them feel less lively, less active, less curious, and less aggressive. Also with the intensity of present-day angling they may well have been pricked, pulled, or hooked and lost; and once bitten twice shy. When such stale fish do take, it is often found that they prefer small flies of sizes 6 to 10. Could this not be the result of a harking back in habit to their prolonged fresh water life as parr, when they fed so keenly on small-sized insects of all sorts? They obviously now have no bodily need to feed; indeed their physical state, coupled with their spasmodic inclination to take, may well be compared to that of a well-fed club habitué who after a good lunch is in no way still hungry or thirsty, but who may succumb to a palatable glass of vintage port, when put before him.

As the spawning time draws nearer, and the water becomes colder, it is also a fact that salmon once more are addicted to taking larger flies or baits, up to three or even four inches long, and ignoring small ones. It is possible that this is due to the emergence of a further instinct hitherto dormant, the urge to protect spawning beds and ova from unwanted intruders. Anyone who has watched salmon spawning in a river well stocked with other sorts of fish will not have failed to notice the crowd of hangers-on at the redd, mainly brown trout and grayling which make a dash for the ova every time that the hen fish shivers herself to release some. The cock salmon will do his best to drive them away, but without more than temporary success. Is it not possible that this protective instinct could have developed both in cock and hen fish some weeks prior to the actual spawning, and that they resent the approach of anything in the shape of a predator, or in the case of the cock salmon a rival? (Male parr can and do fertilise the eggs of hen salmon.) A large fly or bait could resemble such a predator, and the salmon's natural reaction would be to seize it in his mouth, with a view to killing it rather than eating it. This theory may perhaps be far-fetched, and it is only surmise, but it fits in with the evidence and is not unreasonable.

A further possibility is that as the river water temperature in autumn gradually falls back towards the temperature of the sea, it rouses once again in the salmon a memory of his sea feeding habits, so that he preys once again on creatures that in size resemble his previous sea food. Again this is only surmise, but it seems possible.

Another odd circumstance, when one considers it closely, is why when a pool is well stocked with perhaps a hundred or more salmon will only a mere one or two out of that large number take a fly or bait? Logically one would have expected either none at all to take, or else, if one or two, why not twenty or thirty? (That the latter has been known to happen is true, but no one would claim that in Britain it is a common occurrence.)

How often after quickly catching one or two fish in a well-stocked pool has one allowed one's anticipation to rise to heady levels, and how often by the end of a subsequently fruitless day has one descended into the black depths of despondency, not another fish having shown any interest! It may not be logical, but then fishing seldom is.

It may well be that one is lucky to have salmon that will take at all in fresh water. Some types of Pacific salmon are said to refuse all lures once they have entered a river. On the other hand it is fortunate that Atlantic salmon do not take more freely than they actually do, otherwise with the intensive rod fishing of present days there would be few left to carry on the stock.

There are certain conditions of weather or water when salmon are most reluctant to take, e.g. when it is thundery (before the rain falls), when the water is rising fast, when the air is markedly colder than the water, or when the water is polluted or unduly peaty. But under normal circumstances I would hazard a guess that it is the fact that they have already been hooked and lost, or pulled, or pricked that does more than anything to make fish wary. It is often forgotten that by the time they have been in the river only a few weeks the number of lures they have seen may well have run into hundreds, and they are not slow to learn. One notices that fish that have been in the river for some time are much more likely takers after a few days rest than when they are fished over continuously.

Coming Short—How can salmon so frequently pluck and pull at the lure without getting hooked? This is usually known as 'coming short', and why on certain days do they do this time after time? Or if they do become hooked get off quickly?

One day on the Tweed this past autumn I pulled, or hooked, and quickly lost, fourteen fish and only landed three. So far as I could see there was nothing wrong with my tackle or my method of fishing—the previous day with exactly the same outfit and fishing in exactly the same way, I had caught plenty of fish. On this day in question the water was holding a good stock of fish, and was clear and at a good fishing height, though slightly inclined to rise. The barometer was dropping slowly and it rained the next day. However there was no ostensible reason why things should go wrong—but the fish just did not see it that way.

This was a typical example of 'one of those days' which we all meet from time to time. For some reason, often quite inexplicable, fish after fish will just come and pluck at the fly or bait, or get hooked for a few seconds or a minute or two only before dropping off. How on earth do they do it? It makes little difference however sharp are the points of one's hook or however carefully the hooked fish is played. It can be exasperating. Just another pluck, or a few kicks barely turning the reel over, and away he goes again leaving all to be done anew!

That fish are capable of producing this effect when they want to do so is undoubted. The prawn fisherman, too, and to a lesser extent the minnow fisherman, knows it well. When fish are suspicious or cautious and are attracted by the fly or bait, although they know there is something phoney about it, they can come and give it a sharp knock time and again, and still avoid being hooked. It rather reminds one of a dog with a wasp, snapping at it, yet frightened of being stung in the mouth. This may well be a closer parallel than we think, especially in the case of a fish that previously has been pulled or hooked. Undoubtedly too when something indefinable is wrong, and when fish are prone to take in this half-hearted manner, even if they are hooked, it seems that most of them get away.

It is true that there are a number of different ways in which a salmon can give the fly or bait a substantial knock, and they need not necessarily be through his taking it in his mouth.

One day in Iceland on the Vatnsdalsa I was fishing a rocky falls pool from high up on an overhanging cliff. I could see most of the fish in the deep pool below, and they paid no attention to me, seated as I was twenty feet overhead. I was trying a larger fly than usual, a red and black hair winged tube fly of about 2½ inches length. I could watch this fly's path through the water over the fish, also the latter's reaction. I saw one of the bigger fish in the pool rise up towards the fly, as though he was going to take it, but to my surprise when he neared it he turned sharply away and gave it a smart blow with his tail. The resultant pluck on the line was exactly as though a fish had 'come short' and if I had not been able to observe the whole process in the water I would have undoubtedly thus diagnosed it.

Sometimes too, fish try apparently to 'drown' a fly, particularly when it is being fished on a floating line. This can result in their being firmly hooked under the 'chin' and so landed (or lost). Nearly all of us must have caught fish hooked in this way. Anthony Crossley makes particular mention of such episodes in his book *The Floating Line for Salmon and Sea-Trout* (Chapter X). But patently such fish never intend to take the fly into their mouth. Fish behaving in this manner must often give the impression of 'coming short', if the hook point for a moment has touched their exterior but failed to take a hold.

Another way in which fish can give the impression of

'plucking' at the fly is when two flies are being used. A salmon can rise at the dropper but turn away from it at the last moment, and be fouled in some part of his anatomy by the tail fly. This can give the impression of a firm pull, but of course the fish has never taken either fly. If one is unlucky the tail fly may foulhook the fish, and result in a good morning's fishing being lost while one plays him. This happened to me on the Tay one morning with a 27 pounder on light tackle. Although I eventually landed the fish, I lost the best part of a couple of hours good fishing time, and was not best pleased. In this case I clearly saw the fish rise at the bob fly. This sort of thing is a warning that the two flies should not be mounted too close together on the cast. The greater the gap between them, the less the chance of foulhooking with the tail fly, though the chance of the disengaged fly fouling obstructions becomes proportionately increased after a fish has been hooked. One needs in this case a nice sense of proportion when making up the cast.

So there are a number of different ways in which a fish can give the impression of 'coming short' without actually taking the fly into his mouth. Nevertheless these must be of fairly rare occurrence; and no satisfactory explanation has so far been furnished as to why on certain occasions all the offers one gets are of the 'coming short' type, nor why or how fish behave in this way. That there is nothing wrong with one's tackle and manner of fishing can be assumed if both have been substantially successful on the previous day under similar conditions . . . or on second thoughts could there be, in Army terms, some appropriate 'immediate action' that could be taken on such occasions? Remedies might vary under different circumstances, but at least they would be worth some pains of thought. Perhaps a smaller or larger sized fly, or a different type of hook mount might provide a remedy, or a different manner of fishing.

I cannot myself suggest any stock answer to this problem, though if any of my readers can provide one I should be delighted to hear about it from him (or her). In my own case I would, I regret to say, leave the solution to intuition on the spot, an unsatisfying and illogical answer no doubt, but as already noted in this book fishing is seldom logical—and perhaps it is better so!

Before closing these remarks I should mention there is one type of fish which persistently 'comes short', and that is the *running* fish which has just paused on his upstream path long enough to snatch at a fly or bait. More often than not such a fish merely gives a hearty pluck, or if hooked quickly manages to break free. As far as I know there is no answer to this. Nevertheless it should be remembered that appropriate tackle well maintained, coupled with an efficient manner of fishing, and capable handling of hooked fish, will always result in a larger number of fish risen, hooked and landed, both when fish 'come short' or when they are more confiding.

What does a salmon fly represent?

Much controversy has already been aroused by this question. How difficult to give an authoritative answer, and imagination is apt to run riot! In the early days up to Victorian times it was not realized that salmon did not feed in fresh water. They were assumed to behave in much the same way as trout that could be seen feeding at frequent intervals. From Dame Juliana's time (1496) onwards it was apparently considered that salmon in rivers indulged in a varied menu including worms, small fish, caddis, grasshoppers, and flies of all sorts. It was doubtful whether anyone gave the subject much thought. If one wanted to fish for salmon with an artificial fly the obvious answer was to use something akin to a trout fly of accepted pattern, but of greater size mounted on a larger hook in compliment to the salmon's greater bulk. If salmon took such flies, and they sometimes did, that was enough. In subsequent days however if any angler has been asked to set about catching a fish, with the habits of which he is not familiar, surely the first query he will have made is 'what does it feed on?', so that he can imitate such food mounted on a hook. It is worth therefore going back some little way into angling history to discover how bygone authorities viewed the salmon's diet, and how they equated their artificial flies with their findings on this subject.

Going back to 1828, Sir Humphry Davy wrote a well-reasoned and informative book *Salmonia*, and has this to say in it about the salmon's food in fresh water:

> The stomach of the salmon, you will perceive, contains nothing but a little yellow fluid, and, though the salmon is twice as large, does not exceed much in size that of the trout. The stomach of the trout, unlike that of the salmon, will be found full of food . . . I have opened ten or twelve (salmon), and never found anything in their stomachs but tape worms, bred there, and some yellow fluid; but I believe this is generally owing to their being caught at the time of migration, when they are travelling from the sea upwards, and do not willingly load themselves with food.

It seems that Sir Humphry was thus one of the first to observe and record in writing that the salmon was abstemious in fresh water. What then did he imagine salmon flies represented? Presumably river flies, suitably enlarged—or perhaps like many of us even in modern times he did not devote much thought to the subject.

William Scrope in *Days and Nights of Salmon Fishing* (1843) has little to say about salmon feeding in fresh water, though he records having seen a salmon seize a white butterfly as it passed across the water. All the same he was a keen and persistent fly-fisherman.

Thomas Tod Stoddart in his *Anglers Companion to the Rivers and Lochs of Scotland* (1847) cites small fishes, sand-eel, young herring, and shrimp as forming the bulk of a salmon's food in salt water. In this he is no doubt correct up to a point, though there may be much greater variety. In fresh water he largely dodges the issue, saying that the salmon's food and feeding instincts have been 'pretty accurately ascertained', and leaving it at that.

He thus lets this point remain open, but later puts the cart before the horse in implying that because salmon take flies, parr-tails, minnows, and lob-worms when fished, these are what constitute their food; though he is aware that salmon's stomachs very rarely contain anything. He explains this away by the 'quick digestion' theory that the salmon's digestion 'acts like fire' and for that reason no food is ever found inside him. This again is a false idea.

Francis Francis in his *Book on Angling* (1867) writes: 'I may say that I have seen salmon feed greedily on the little eels, which during the "eel fare" run up rivers. These facts, combined with their taking both worm and minnow, when they can get it, quite assure me that the notion that salmon do not feed when in fresh water, which so generally prevails, is extremely incorrect. Salmon perhaps do not feed very voraciously, because in salmon rivers, as a general rule, food, and particularly in the heavy waters salmon inhabit, is not very abundant, and the salmon is not given to roaming about far from home in search of food; but I very much question whether anything passes his lair within eye-shot, which is at all worth his notice, that he does not take stock or toll of.' So Francis undoubtedly believed that salmon fed in the river, though he does not mention river flies as part of their diet.

Kelson in *The Salmon Fly* (1895) was quite certain that salmon fed in fresh water and he had actually seen them doing it. He wrote: 'At last I had distinct ocular proof (with the aid of field glasses) that salmon feed on flies, moths, wasps, and caterpillars, as well as on their own species. But this is not all, for after baiting clear places for the purpose, I have seen them pick up prawns . . .'. If however he thought that the 250 or so ornate patterns of fly described in his book represented natural insects he must have had a very vivid imagination.

P. D. Malloch in *Tay Salmon and Other Fish* (1908) was one of the first authorities to state that salmon definitely absorbed no nourishment during their sojourn in fresh water, neither before nor after spawning; and Sir Herbert Maxwell in his introduction to a new 1920 edition of Francis Francis' *Book on Angling* stated categorically that salmon did not feed in fresh water.

So eventually the truth was reached with regard to salmon's fresh water feed, or rather the absence of it; but still the issue was not clear in some people's minds because salmon could be seen rising to March Brown or Mayfly, also they could be caught on worms.

However, as no doubt the observant reader will have

noticed, the question of whether salmon feed or not in fresh water is only a side issue to the question of what a salmon fly represents. If we knew exactly the salmon's diet in the sea, we could surely devise flies to imitate certain items in it. It is true we are now getting nearer to answering this question. We know well enough what the parr eats, also the smolt as long as he is in fresh water, i.e. most types of aquatic insect or fish life small enough for him to swallow. In the sea we *know* that herrings and sand eels are part of the adolescent or adult salmon's diet, and we can assume that he eats the capelin which abound in the north-west Atlantic, and also, from his pink flesh, that he feeds abundantly on some form of crustacean. We also know that the salmon in salt water feeds voraciously, because nothing else would produce his so-rapid growth.

Is it therefore taking it too far to assume that while in the sea he is to all intents and purposes omnivorous and feeds on whatever forms of small marine life (apart perhaps from the more obnoxious forms of squid, jelly fish and the like) that he can catch and swallow? Such a diet must vary to a large extent, depending on where he happens to find himself; e.g. very different, one would expect, in the Bay of Biscay from in the Davis Straits for example. And it must also vary according to his state of growth, in that a five-inch smolt would not be expected to eat the same type and amount of food as a 30-pound salmon. His food during his sea life of one, two or three years would therefore seem to be widely diversified.

But the question is: does the modern salmon fly represent any particular item in such a diet? It has been suggested that Vulturine Guinea-Fowl flies represent elvers, Jock Scotts the Striped Wrasse, Silver Greys young herrings, Red Sandys the deep sea crustacean, Spey flies such as the Lady Caroline, Black Heron, or Purple King the off-shore prawn or shrimp, and very small flies plankton.

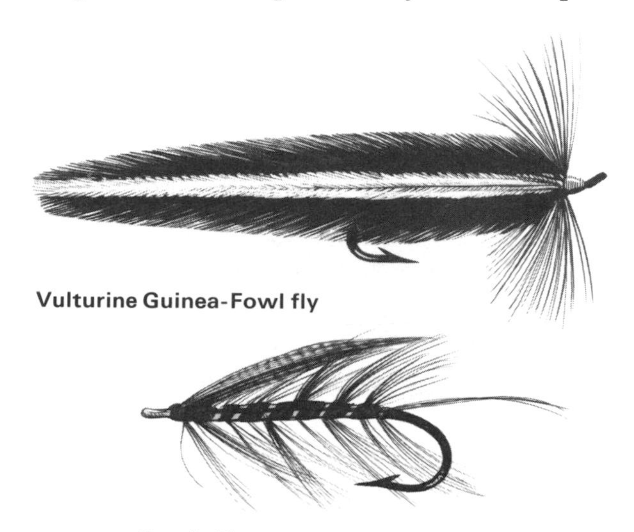

Vulturine Guinea-Fowl fly

Purple King

This may possibly be the case, but if so it is more by accident than design. Does anyone suppose for instance that when Jock Scott on his voyage to Norway in 1845 made up the original prototype of his famous fly that he was painstakingly imitating the wrasse? The idea is ridiculous. Nor does the blue and white striped Vulturine Guinea-Fowl feather, apart from its length, in any way resemble the elver which it is supposed to represent. (Polar bear hair would give a far better imitation.)

To digress for a moment, will the reader pause to consider the case of worms in Iceland? The worm is an outstandingly popular bait for salmon amongst Icelandic anglers, and tens of thousands of salmon are caught on it every season. One might think there was nothing extraordinary about this, if one did not know that there are by nature no worms in the volcanic Icelandic soil, and that all those used for bait are bought from a worm farm near Reykjavik, the stock for which is imported from abroad! So although no Icelandic salmon has never seen a worm before, this does not stop him from taking it greedily. The fact that it is alive, looks or smells good, is not too big a prey, and reminds him of some previous food unspecified is enough.

So in the case of salmon flies the answer surely must be that if the salmon is largely omniverous, until we discover that he has some particular predilection for some special form of food, it does not greatly matter what a fly represents, apart from it being something lifelike.

It is possible also that, if flies sufficiently small are used, they may arouse a reaction in the salmon's mind derived from his feeding habits in parr life (this sounds a more rational explanation than that they represent plankton!).

So, finally, one might conclude (until further detailed knowledge becomes available) that a salmon fly represents:

(i) Something alive, i.e. being fished in such a way as to give the illusion of lifelike motion, helped by the movement of hackles and other feathers or hair in the stream.

(ii) Something of a suitable size for a salmon to prey on.

(iii) If small, some minor form of freshwater life, akin to the prey of the parr and smolt.

(iv) If larger, some form of marine life on which the salmon has fed during his sojourn in the sea, such food being of many different varieties, about many of which we are still uncertain.

(v) In the case of an upstream dry-fly or an upstream nymph (the use of which in Britain is rare), the food eaten by the salmon during his parr-life in the river, as in (iii) above.

(vi) n.b. As the breeding season approaches from mid-September onwards, a large fly may represent some creature of which the salmon is jealous (e.g. a cock parr), or else some small fish or other creature from which his (or her) instinct is to protect the ova. Admittedly this is descending towards the realms of speculation and putting the cart before the horse; but it is noticeable:

(a) That cock parr will fertilise the ova of hen salmon, and so might arouse jealousy in the cock salmon.

(b) That brown trout and other fish feed greedily on the hen salmon's ova.

(c) That the cock salmon on or near the redd makes persistent efforts to chase away such intruders.

So that if in autumn one fishes with a lure of 3 or 4 inches long, sufficiently sizeable to imitate one of these intruders, one might expect the adult salmon to adopt aggressive action towards it. If it refuses to swim away one could expect this action to consist of a bite (or possibly a sharp slap with the tail).

To go further than this, into what a salmon fly represents, in our present state of knowledge must be pure speculation; and without more detailed and trustworthy information is not justifiable.

2
Enemies of the Salmon

The enemies of the Salmon are many, both in the sea and in fresh water. It is worth giving a good deal of thought to them in these days when our salmon stocks are so much at risk, and to the means by which the harm they do can be limited.

All through their life from the ova to the kelt stage salmon like most wild creatures are continually at risk. Both in the sea and in rivers there is little doubt that man is the chief predator. It would be a simple matter for man to exterminate Atlantic salmon in any given river, by the deliberate action of extending a series of nets from bank to bank or else by indiscriminate and continuous trapping or netting, and by leistering or stroke-hauling off the spawning beds—this, quite apart from indirect destructive processes initiated by him, such as pollution, erection of impassable obstructions, water abstraction and the like. In the sea too, as we all know, the salmon in his migratory path is preyed upon by man's long lines, drift nets, and coastal nets. This is a comparatively new development, and the salmon now seems to have little security anywhere.

The ravages of mankind can only be checked by the wise control and protective measures enforced by fellow men in possession of the necessary authority and the ability to exercise it. When these fail the salmon perishes—witness what has happened in France, Spain, Ireland, and

New England. All these countries would have salmon in overflowing abundance, but for the destruction caused by man in the past. England too has nothing about which to congratulate itself on this score, nor has Norway (though the situation is no doubt becoming better there with the 50 mile sea limit and the recent prohibition of fresh water netting and trapping). Scotland, Canada and Iceland alone seem to have pursued a wiser path, and in other countries the responsible authorities in this matter could rightly have been likened to sleep-walkers on a window-sill, beyond the edge—beyond also the point of recovery.

However it is not the purpose of this chapter to go further into the destructive practices of mankind nor into the remedial measures for these already undertaken in the past or proposed for the future. This subject is so complex and widespread that it would require a separate volume. It does seem worthwhile however to take a brief look at the creatures in fish, animal and bird life which prey upon salmon, and make some estimate of the amount of harm they do, coupled with suggestions about their control or otherwise.

Starting in the sea, there are no doubt a large and varied number of predators where salmon are concerned, at all stages from the smolt to the fully mature adult fish. At one end of the scale we find killer-whales and sharks. Anthony Crossley, for instance, in his *Floating Line for Salmon and Sea-Trout* cites the case of three sharks caught in the North Sea, one of which had ten salmon inside it, one eight, and one three. No doubt such creatures prey frequently on adult fish, but killer-whales admittedly also eat seals (another salmon predator), so this may to some extent balance their bad record. Porpoises are another danger to salmon. It does not seem likely however that any restriction on the number of these creatures could be effected.

Where seals are concerned, however, far more incisive action could be taken. The present number of grey seals round British coasts is reliably estimated as 15,000. Common seals in addition number around 10,000. Grey seals are estimated to eat 15lb. of fish per day and common seals some 10lb. This brings the total weight of British fish eaten by seals each year to around 50,000 tons—a horrifying aggregate.

What proportion of this total consists of salmon and grilse seeking their parent river is difficult to estimate, but even if it is put as low as 2 per cent (and one would have thought this a conservative estimate) it means that as high a weight of salmon and grilse as 1000 tons is eaten by seals every year, or over 280,000 fish in number (at an average weight of 8lb. per fish). In addition a further number of fish are injured by seal bites and though not eaten subsequently die. This is made clear by the large number of fish caught, both by net and rod, which carry seal bites of varying severity. They are not scarce.

Surely here there is a crying need for substantial reduction of the number of seals round our coasts. No-one would want seals to be exterminated, but it seems that few people realize the extent of their inroads on fish stocks of all sorts, not only salmon, merciless predators as they are. There is nothing off British coasts, apart it is to be supposed from a very occasional shark or killer whale, that preys on them. It is a pity in this respect that like Greenland we don't run to a fair stock of polar bears! And unless the necessary steps are taken it must be assumed that our seals will continue to increase in numbers and will consume a still higher proportion of our fish, including salmon and grilse.

There is a wide variety of other sea creatures that prey on immature salmon at least. We may not know them all. Some of them are coal fish, cod, pollack, and conger eels which will certainly eat smolts or small immature grilse whenever they have the chance. They may well gather near river mouths to await the descending smolts. It would seem that little could be done to reduce their numbers.

In fresh water adult salmon have few enemies, apart from humans. Otters take an occasional fish, but apart from their being charming animals their numbers are far too few nowadays to cause any perceptible loss to fish stocks and they should be left in peace. Pike if very large could swallow grilse or small salmon, and no doubt do so. But again the numbers of pike large enough to attempt this must be small. Incidentally it may interest the reader to know that a 27lb. pike caught by electric fishing on the Dorset Frome last year had inside it an 8lb. kelt. Also on the Blackwater in Co. Cork the author has on a number of occasions seen pike of 20lb. and bigger which would be capable without difficulty of taking kelts or salmon up to 9lb. at least. Such fish must take a fair toll. But a far more substantial loss must be the number of parr and smolts eaten by pike of all sizes. These could run into many thousands in any river where pike are numerous, and these predators should be ruthlessly destroyed by every possible means.

Another enemy of salmon, often tolerated or overlooked, is the brown trout. Any brown trout of ¾lb. or bigger will eat parr and smolts, which they do in large numbers. They also eat salmon ova at spawning time, and young trout compete with fry, parr, and smolts, for the available food and living space. Most salmon rivers hold brown trout in varying numbers. The Tweed for instance has a big stock of them. The Dee on the other hand is fortunate in possessing relatively few. It is impossible to calculate the amount of harm which brown trout cause to salmon stocks, but they must be among the worst villains in the piece. It seems a most misguided policy, as is sometimes done, to stock a salmon river with brown trout in the first place, and if in addition it is also stocked with salmon fry or parr the two processes would seem contradictory.

Sea trout so far as salmon are concerned are little better associates than brown trout, and for the same reasons. They are present in the river through most of the year, if their kelt period is taken into account—but they often spawn lower down in the river system than do the majority of the salmon, so perhaps on that account they do less harm.

Such other fish as chub, grayling, perch and eels all do harm to a limited extent. Eels are perhaps the worst of these, being ceaselessly on the move by night rather than by day. They eat ova fry and parr whenever they get the chance, but fortunately are likely to be hibernating at spawning time, so would be less destructive to ova than some other types of fish. But none of these fish are welcome denizens of a salmon river, and all are better removed in so far as anyone is prepared to take the trouble to do this.

Birds too account for many immature salmon from the fry stage onwards. Ospreys and divers are too rare to cause any worry, but cormorants are another matter. Though no doubt they will swallow any type of sizeable fish, they doubtless prey heavily on parr and smolts. Goosanders and mergansers are as bad or worse. One July when my friends and I were fishing on the Spey we saw a number of mergansers diving and fishing in the pool below us; so we took our guns and shot three or four of them. Opening them up we found them stuffed with salmon parr, up to 27 parr inside one of them. There were no small trout or other fish amongst these. One can amuse oneself estimating what would be the total number of salmon parr eaten by a single merganser at this rate during the course of the year; and then multiplying the resulting figure by the total number of mergansers one reckons inhabit the river catchment area. The result is alarming—approaching a seven figure number on the bigger rivers, and it makes one wonder whether it would not be simpler and less expensive to organize a wholesale destruction of mergansers, by shooting and other methods, rather than run to the expense and labour involved in a hatchery. The parr thus preserved might come near to equalling in numbers the output from a hatchery and they would be wild parr with a better survival rate than tame hatchery specimens.

Herons and gulls must also take their toll of parr and smolts, as also would terns of fry or small parr. But it is a fascinating sight watching terns hovering and diving on their prey, and no one would want to harm the lovely 'sea swallows', even if he had no compunction in downing the murderous black back.

It could no doubt be argued that inroads on salmon stocks by many of the above predators are not as serious as they might at first appear to be, because of the omnivorous nature of many of the latter.

For instance if mergansers eat salmon parr they doubtless also eat small brown trout and sea trout, which themselves compete with or later prey on salmon fry and parr. The same could be said about herons and cormorants, even pike and other fish, so to a certain extent the harm done is offset by an indirect gain. But even if this is true, one feels that the destruction of the original predators would be a better safeguard; and in the case of seals and brown trout there would seem to be no redeeming features (except of course in the view of the brown trout fishers!).

Once again, to conclude this chapter, it should be emphasized that the salmon's arch-enemy above all others, if given a free-hand, is mankind. None of his natural foes in the form of animal, fish, or bird life, as listed above, even when combined could bring about his downfall. In fact, if it was only them he had to contend with, he would doubtless come out on top in the way of greatly increased numbers. It is solely the unchecked ravages of man which could spell his doom.

The jump of a fresh salmon, probably resting. As for a kelt, quite apart from its thin appearance, its jump makes much less of a splash and is not so impressive.

II

WATERSIDE CONDITIONS

Pushing on. The jump of a running fish.

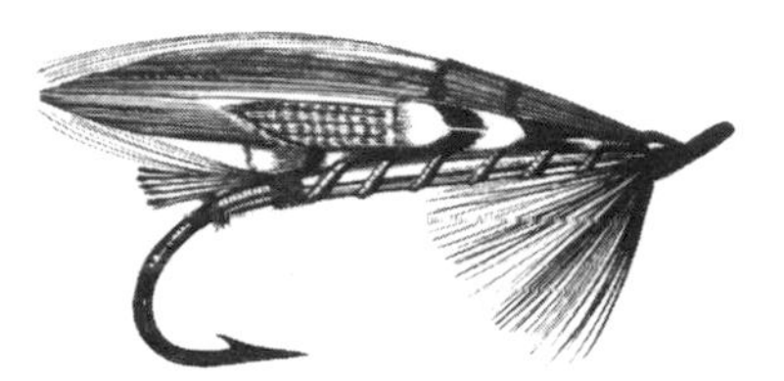

The old

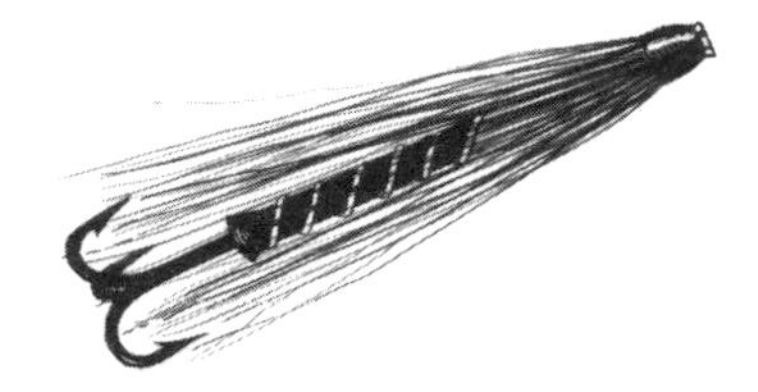

and the new

3
Water and Air Temperature

A salmon is what we term a 'cold blooded' creature, with the result that he always maintains his body temperature within a degree or so of that of the water which surrounds him. In this way his reaction to changes in the temperature of his environment differs completely from that of a warm blooded creature, such as a healthy human being, whose blood temperature remains the same whether the air around him is below freezing point or at 120°F. Although river or lake water temperature, compared to that of air, changes slowly, its variation in Britain is a wide one of approximately 45°F. This in turn means that the body and blood temperature of our salmon while in fresh water is liable to a similar variation, which he can successfully endure (whereas as we all know the human body can compete with no more than about 12°F variation). It is not surprising therefore that salmon's behaviour changes markedly between extremes of temperature from near freezing point to 78 or so degrees Fahrenheit.

As well as being directly influenced by water temperature, the salmon is also affected by air temperature in some curious and indirect way. If anyone doubts this let him consider the immediate beneficial effect on fishing of a sudden warm spell during an otherwise cold and bitter spring day. While the cold persists not a fish has shown interest in the angler's lure, but with half an hour's bright warm sunshine on such a day, maybe two or three fish at once take hold. Yet the water, except possibly in the surface layer, will have undergone no change in temperature during such a short period, unlike the air which may have warmed by 10°F or more. This change in air temperature however will somehow have communicated itself to the fish, which is both curious and interesting.

Water temperature changes much slower than air temperature, but in the long run is governed by it. This has a direct effect on fishing because for some reason, not easy to explain, fish always take better when the air is warmer than the water. This holds good throughout the whole range of water temperatures, but it is most marked when the water is cold, say at 42°F or less. When air and water are the same in temperature fish take almost equally well. They will still take passably well, though with more reluctance, with the air only a degree or two colder than the water. But when it falls to five degrees or more colder, they will seldom take. (A sunk lure then offers the best chance.)

Incidentally it should be noted in passing that this unfavourable contrast in water and air temperature holds good equally with the water temperature anywhere between 70°F and 33°F. It is a disadvantage all along the line. The only place I have so far found where it can be ignored is Iceland. I have often seen fish caught there in numbers on a floating line with the air temperature as much as 10°F lower than that of the water. But Iceland salmon as a rule are exceptionally ready takers. I also remember catching a salmon on the Tweed at Rutherford one November evening many years ago when it was freezing so bitterly that I could not stop the line freezing inextricably in the rod rings while I was playing the fish. I kept it moving in and out all the time, being well aware of what was happening, and kept the reel turning this way and that to avoid that also being frozen solid. But all to no avail; after six or seven minutes everything became immovable, so that I had to walk backwards with about thirty yards of line out, until Brown, my boatman, could net my fish onto the bank. This happened in a pool called Between the Caulds if any of my readers know it. There must have been a good fifteen degrees of adverse difference in water and air temperatures on that occasion, so perhaps this was one of those exceptions that prove the rule. Brown said afterwards that it took an hour in front of his fire for my reel to thaw out! I only relate this story as illustrating one of those unusual instances which prove nothing except that no rules in fishing are inviolate.

To summarize, if the reader will bear with me, it might be worth while making a short resumé of the general effects on salmon of the varying heights of water temperature, and of the salmon's corresponding behaviour, as follows:
(Figures of temperature and time are naturally only approximate, but give a reasonably accurate guide).

Water Temperature	
32°F–37°F	Fish will take passably well, water colour and height being favourable, for a few hours from 11 a.m. onwards, when the air temperature is at its warmest. They prefer large sized baits or flies. It is of little use fishing much before 11 a.m. Fish do not seem to 'wake up' till then, after the

long hours of cold and dark inactivity.

Fish are often unwilling to enter rivers from the sea, which is perhaps six or more degrees warmer than fresh water. Also having entered rivers, they are reluctant to run fast or far in this temperature of water. They will halt at any substantial fall or obstacle, which later they will probably surmount without hesitation. They prefer deep quiet water in which to lie, and avoid shallows and rapids. When hooked, fresh salmon are apt to put up a poor fight, giving the impression of being partly numbed with the cold.

38°F–43°F

The same remarks as above apply, though to a lesser degree. Fish will usually take well at this temperature, though large sized flies fished on a sinking line, and fairly large baits are still appropriate. Some fish begin to move into streamier water, though most of them still prefer to lie in the slacker and deeper pools. The fresh water temperature in spring will now be approaching that of the sea, so the entry of fish should be more extensive; also fish will move higher upstream in the rivers.

44°F–49°F

These temperatures produce what is definitely an upturn in the behaviour of fish. River temperatures are now likely to be higher than that of the sea, and no bar to fish entering fresh water. Also fish will now attempt to surmount any obstacle which they may find in fresh water, in the way of falls, weirs, etc. These are good taking temperatures, and fish should take freely. Fish will also show, either by jumping or head and tailing, much more frequently in rivers. Some of them will permeate right to headwaters. Sunk line fishing with largish flies or bait casting with medium sized baits are still the most effective methods.

50°F–56°F

With these temperatures the floating line has come into its own, not necessarily with the smallest flies, but with those of anywhere between size 4 and size 8. In rapid streams, big flies of two to three inches length can still be effective. Again this is a very good 'taking' temperature. There is no need now to fall back on the use of a sinking line, not even in time of spate. Fish will run freely, and some will reach the furthest upstream reaches of any river system. Flies skating, or 'dibbed' across the surface of the water begin to become effective. In some rivers with very clear water, such as the Aberdeenshire Dee, small flies of sizes 8–10 may be useful. These temperatures provide perhaps the best range for the fly fisher's activities.

57°–63°F

Such temperatures are getting warmer than one would like. However they are by no means a bar to fish taking. Fresh run salmon and grilse will almost certainly now prefer shallower streams, and this is where they should be sought. Both fly and bait (if it is used) should be greatly reduced in size, a number 6 fly being a substantial size under these conditions. The fly should be fished near or on the surface. Fish now prefer the streamy stretches of the river, and any that linger in the deep holes will probably be old stagers that can well be ignored.

64°F–70°F or over

These temperatures herald a fishing stumer. Up to 70°F it is still quite possible to attract fish to a fly or bait, particularly if they are fresh run. But when the water temperature reaches 70°F or higher, fish start to have a wholetime struggle to survive, and will pay little attention to lures of any sort. The only exceptions are fresh-run fish with sea-lice, if any are encountered under such conditions. (A temperature of this height implies a heat-wave with a dead-low river, which it is unlikely that fish will enter from the sea; or if they do they will almost certainly be caught in estuary nets).

At these high temperatures a certain number of dead or dying fish will be found. Any temperature of over 70°F is liable to be lethal to salmon, and some are bound to succumb. The majority of fish will gather in the deeper holes, and can often be seen in shoals there, as it were gasping for breath. At dusk they may move into the streams, and here is where any fresh-run ones are likely to be found. A water temperature of 75°F is about as high as is likely to be experienced in British salmon rivers, and that but seldom. In any case when it is over 65°F fishing is certain to deteriorate.

There are various other points in connection with water temperatures and their effect on fishing which are well worth noting. One is as follows. When the river is pretty warm, say at 60°F–65°F and well stocked with fish that are becoming 'potted', a sudden drop in temperature, of four or five degrees, is as good as a spate in putting them on the take. Such a drop in temperature seldom occurs, but overnight frost higher up the river can cause it, or a sudden downpour of rain. The effect is not likely to last for more than a day, so the resultant opportunity should not be missed.

As to changes in temperature, it is better on the whole that they should be gradual rather than too sudden. As explained previously the salmon's metabolism is closely connected with water temperature, and too quick a change either to warmer or colder upsets him, or at least puts him off the take. I have seen the Spey in May (a good fishing month) quickly rise in basic water temperature by ten or twelve degrees Fahrenheit, due presumably to a warm sun playing upon its slow running upper reaches in the neighbourhood of Aviemore and Loch Insh. Such a rise in temperature seems to distract the attention of the fish, and is apt to put them off the take for a day or two. Another place where quick rises in temperature can have a bad effect is Iceland. In July there the normal water temperature is 45°–52°F. But hot sun within a day or so can quickly raise this to 60°F or higher. This is particularly noticeable in a river that runs through a shallow lake, as many of them do; and it is the one factor there which can and does temporarily cause fish to take less well.

It is also worth noting the different reaction of spring fish and autumn fish to varying basic levels in water temperature. Spring fish take best as a rule when the thermometer shows between 44°F and 58°F. That is they seem to like the water to be reasonably warm. Autumn fish on the other hand (and I am referring to the fresh-run fish of October and November, not to old potted spring and summer fish), definitely take best with the water at 45°F or colder. They will take freely with its temperature at 37°F to 40°F, or even when colder, but much less freely if it is at around 50°F. Why this should be so I can offer no explanation, unless it is that the colder temperatures turn the fish's mind towards spawning, and prompt him to attack possible ova-predators before they can do any harm. In any case it seems to be in direct contrast to the behaviour of spring fish which tend to be more active in taking as the water warms, and more sluggish as it chills.

One other point about water temperature, it is the general rise in this which more than anything else causes kelts to leave the river for the sea. Kelts will outstay floods and changes in water level. They will even move upstream at times in company with fresh-run salmon. But let the basic water temperature rise to somewhere around 48°F and they will disappear as though by magic. It is a relief to be rid of them, though a pity that more of them do not survive to augment a later run of returning fresh-fish.

On the crucial subject of water temperatures, I hope the foregoing may have been of occasional interest here and there. It seems to me it is usually worth including a pocket thermometer in one's fishing kit, although these have a horrible habit of getting lost or broken. The temperature of the water, together with its height, is one of the first pieces of information one seeks on arrival on a new water. It is a factor that always has an immediate bearing on one's fishing, and it should invariably be borne in mind. After the initial verification one can probably form an accurate enough estimate of any changes by dipping one's hand below the surface. In this as in other aspects of fishing it is often a relief not to be dependent on the instruments of modern science!

4
Water Height and Strength

As a whole salmon prefer to lie in water of about four foot to eight foot in depth. This is a general estimate both for rivers and lochs, though it is true that in the cold water of spring they prefer slightly deeper and slacker water, up to around twelve or fourteen feet deep. In summer, with warm water, some of them will venture into quite shallow streams of perhaps three feet depth or even less, in order presumably to benefit from a higher oxygen content.

In spite of their beautifully streamlined shape, salmon do not like to lie in fast streams for any length of time. The effort is too great; as when they are spending anything up to twelve months in fresh water, without feeding, the need to conserve energy is obviously a pressing one. Where salmon are seen consistently jumping in fast water, and thus apparently lying there, it is certain that the bottom is broken and that some big boulders or other sunken obstructions are giving them shelter against the stream. In addition it should be remembered that the low level current of a river, where it is continuously being checked by boulders or other obstructions on the river-bed, will be running at an appreciably slower speed than the surface current.

When the river rises in height after rain or melting snow fish will come close in to the bank, provided depth and speed of water are suitable. I always remember a certain ghillie on the Spey, who in a high and coloured water would demonstrate how to catch salmon in a landing-net by running it down the bank and walking quickly downstream with it, held close to the bottom as well as to the bank. Fish that had taken refuge from the flood by drawing close in under the bank would dart out and into the net when it was thus handled. He caught one as big as about 27lb. by this method one day. Needless to say all fish so caught were returned unharmed to the water.

That rising water usually encourages fish to run is undoubtedly a truism, as can be verified at any weir or cauld where fish can be seen mounting. Nevertheless it cannot invariably be true in the case of every fish, as the headwaters of any river system would obviously be soon choked with them, if they ran as fast and far as they could on every rise of river. There must be a limit on the distance upstream which they are prepared to run; presumably this is bounded by the location of the spawning beds which they are seeking, where they themselves originally were bred. For instance some of the autumn fish in Spey, Tay and Tweed will persist in remaining low down the river to spawn in that neighbourhood, and in the tributaries there, however many the floods or rises in water which they may experience.

With any rise in water, fish that have already run their requisite distance up-river will merely take shelter somewhere out of the main current and await a fall in water level before moving back to their normal lies.

In a very big flood some salmon will even drop a fair distance downstream. Spey netsmen for instance say they often catch a number of stale fish, that have obviously been in fresh water for some time, in the aftermath of any big spate during the summer. A downstream movement of this sort is likely, one would have thought, to take place in any part of a fast running river after an unusually high spate, and not just in the lowest reaches. Rising water is usually considered a bugbear for anglers. It is true that it appears to distract the salmon's attention and render him unresponsive to any sort of lure; nevertheless it is perhaps not always such a complete drawback as is imagined. Where there is a fall or a weir, difficult of ascent, some fish are certain to pause in their upstream passage, particularly when they are tired after a long run.

They may well pause either downstream of the obstacle, or just as likely upstream after surmounting it. And where they stop even temporarily there is always a fair chance that they will take. So in a rising water the angler should concentrate on such places; and he should not leave them unless he has to, because at such a time there is more than ever the likelihood of new fish arriving and stopping there.

A quick rise in water is bad. With the river colouring fast, and with a succession of branches, and debris of all sorts being carried downstream, the angler is unlikely to miss anything if he retires to the fireside, or goes to visit ruined castles or the local race meeting. If however the rise is slow, say at a rate of an inch every two hours, or four or five inches during the course of the day, this does not seem to matter nearly so much; some fish, perhaps a good number, will certainly still take. One of the best days we ever had on the Cork Blackwater, when four of us caught thirty-nine fish for the day, was when, in the course of the day, the water rose five inches.

Again at the very start of a rise, perhaps before its imminence has become apparent to the angler, fish will often take well. At such a time, as soon as he realizes what is afoot, the angler if he has a good pool at his disposal, holding plenty of fish, would do well to go and fish at once in the very neck of it, and remain there. Fish preparing to run, are likely at a time like this to push up into such a neck; and two or three more may well be caught there before the flood water arrives to put a halt to the proceedings. This again is an opportunity that occurs not infrequently, and as it is likely to be short lived it should be quickly appreciated.

5
Effects of Light

Light, without doubt, has a considerable effect on the success or otherwise of salmon fishing; its degree of strength and its character should be a permanent consideration, conscious or unconscious, in the back of the successful fisherman's mind.

Light relevant to salmon fishing is sunlight, direct, diffused, or reflected. For one reason or another, as we all know, a bright sun, unveiled by clouds and shining with intensity from high in the heavens directly down on the water to be fished, is a grave disadvantage for the angler. Why this should be so is not so obvious. Sunlight seems to stir some forms of life into action, such as insects and birds. Animals and human beings however, in bright hot sun often become somnolent. Perhaps fish react in the same way? They have no eyelids to shut out the light from their eyes, and all other creatures go to sleep at intervals, so why not fish? In any case it is most noticeable, if on a bright summer day one watches a pool that is holding a good stock of fish, how in the early morning before the sun has risen high there may well be plenty of activity, with fish showing and moving everywhere; but after half an hour or less of full sunshine, torpor seems to descend, and not a fish now shows where previously they had been so active. This is curious, but of course it only applies when the water is reasonably warm. When it is cold, say at 46°F or less, warm sunshine often encourages activity.

I have often wondered why it is that a bright sun should be such a handicap to one's fishing efforts. There are many explanations to be heard from time to time. It is said that bright sunshine makes one's tackle, such of it as is visible to fish, show up so obviously that it becomes patently unnatural, and fish are thus deterred from taking. It is also said that the shadow of one's line cast and fly exercise a similar deterrent effect, and I have already mentioned the torpor that appears to descend on fish when the summer sun shines brightly—irrespective of whether they are being fished over or not.

Fish are shy creatures, and a big fish like a salmon is closely confined in any river except one of the largest.

He has all the wild creature's permanent sense of 'qui vive' with regard to possible enemies. Perhaps the bright sun shining without restraint upon him has the same effect as a searchlight illuminating a patrol of infantry in wartime no-man's land. The immediate reaction in both cases could be similar, to keep down and make no movement which could draw unwelcome attention. Another likelihood is that a warm sun shining directly on already warm water can quickly cause the water temperature to rise to a level which begins to become unacceptable to fish. In certain cases this could well be relevant. When the water reaches a temperature of 70°F or over it seems that the struggle to obtain enough oxygen from it becomes the dominant consideration for the fish, and all superfluous activity comes to a stop.

None of these expanations however seems by itself to be entirely convincing—though probably it is a combination of all of them which approaches nearest to the truth.

The direction of the sunlight is another factor of importance. A sun shining directly downstream always seems bad for fishing, whether high in the sky or low. So is a sun shining directly upstream; but crossways from either side is not nearly so bad. It is hard to find a reason for this. As the salmon's eyes are at the side of his head one would have thought an upstream or downstream sun might have been less distracting, but it does not seem so. It may be noted at this juncture that although the spring sun may appear to be shining brightly, its rays are usually much less strong than those of the summer sun, as a light meter will confirm. There must be more clarity in the summer atmosphere.

There is no doubt that when the sun is bright it pays to fish streamy ripply water, and to leave the flats and smooth glides untouched. Fish in such fast streams will often take, when in the smooth water they become quite uncatchable.

This would seem to support the theory that the shadow of line and leader puts them off. In rapids there will of course be a shadow from every ripple, and extra ones will not be apparent. In calm water however the shadow from line and monofilament on the bottom will be easily distinguishable, as there will be nothing to camouflage it; and this could well frighten a fish or at least distract his attention. It is said too that a floating line throws a much wider shadow than a sunk one, owing to the surface disturbance which accompanies it. All this may well be true, and to try to fish smooth water in bright sun may well do more harm than good. No doubt it is far better to rest such water until better conditions prevail. It has been recommended that in bright sun a longer leader than normal should be used, say of twelve feet instead of nine, the idea being to keep the substance and shadow of the thick dressed line further from the fly. This too can do no harm, provided the rod is long enough to cast such a leader adequately; but all the same I doubt whether it really makes much difference. A sunk line and sunk fly even if of small size, on the other hand, can prove surprisingly successful on a bright day. I have witnessed this more than once. Perhaps such an outfit scores by throwing less shadow on the bottom, or by being more easily accessible to the fish. 'Dibbing' the fly along the surface is another way of competing with the sun. Fish will sometimes take a fly fished in this way when they will look at nothing else, and bright sun especially in ripply water does not necessarily put them off. Even a dry-fly can be tried in bright sunlight, not without hope (see chapter 13). In fact a really warm air temperature is apparently an asset for this form of fishing. One point should not be overlooked on a bright day. Do not let your shadow or that of your companion fall over any smooth surface water that you intend to fish. While it matters little if the water is broken and ripply, the shadow of a human being or a fishing rod passing over a glassy surface will carry right down to the bottom, and is likely to cause fish to move away if it passes over them; and the shallower the water the worse the effect.

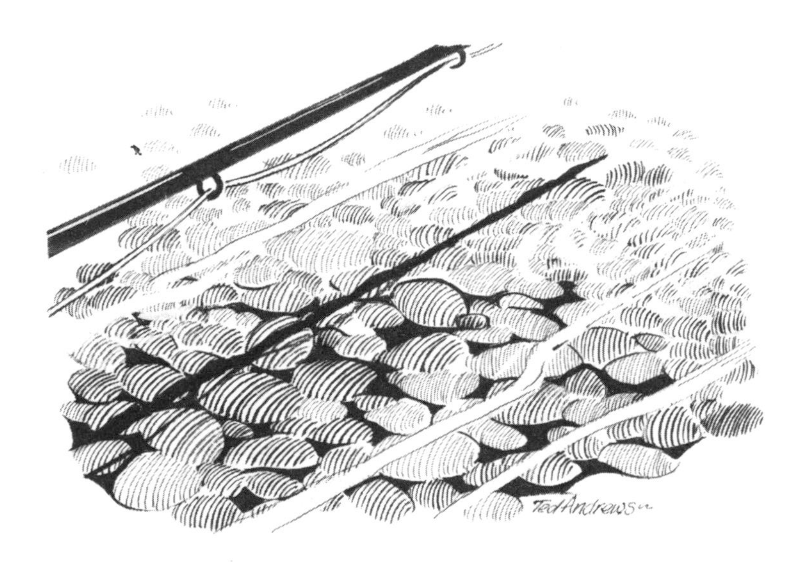

If the water is coloured after a spate, the particles in it producing discolouration act to some extent as a light filter, so bright sun is not so harmful to fishing at such a time. Nor in the cold water of early spring or autumn is the sunshine such a handicap. As already pointed out the sun's rays are in any case by nature less penetrating at this time of year, and their warmth does good rather than harm by livening up both fish and fisherman.

After a hot summer's day it sometimes happens that there is a brilliant sunset producing a strong red glow in the west when the sun is down. One has heard it asserted that it is quite useless to fish while a glow of this type persists; and if one questions the validity of this claim one may be fobbed off with the story that it is due to the presence of infra-red rays, or some nonsense of the sort. I do not believe this for a moment; and as one seldom seems to be exposed to a glow of this type (there is usually a high bank or a hill-side in the way), this would not seem to be a factor of great importance. If in fact fishing does suffer from the presence of such a red glow, of which I am not fully convinced, I would rather attribute this to the air after sunset cooling down quickly, while the water is left warm after a hot summer's day. This would produce unfavourable conditions for fishing, and is a more rational explanation for fish becoming dour at such a time, rather than anything to do with the glowing red light of sunset.

Turning from conditions of bright sunlight to dull dim or cloudy weather, with the light for one reason or another subdued, we find that the effect on fishing is mixed. Twilight for instance, in reasonably warm weather, is good whether at dawn or dusk. During hot summer weather it is delightful to start fishing in the early morning before the bright sunshine by about eleven a.m. bathes everything in its glare. It is also without doubt the most profitable time of day for fishing under such conditions. Five a.m. is not too early to start, unless you are unlucky and choose a morning when the air is colder than usual and the river as a result is exuding thick vapour. This does occur unexpectedly from time to time, and in such circumstances it will be of little use fishing until the air has warmed up enough to cause the mist to disappear.

Twilight in evening is also a good light for fishing, always provided that the air temperature does not quickly fall after sundown so as to become appreciably lower than that of the water. Normally our evenings are reasonably warm and continue so for a fair period until darkness. Fishing in the half light can then prove highly successful. It seems that as the light starts to fail fish become more lively and enterprising, as they do also in the half light of a summer's morning. This is confirmed at such establishments where a watch is kept on the passage of fish through salmon ladders. Apart from a time of rising water or spate, or when the water is unduly cold, the greatest activity amongst salmon pushing upstream always takes place in early morning or in the evening, when daylight is subdued.

Mention has already been made of mist rising off the water. Such a mist in itself is not adverse, but as has been pointed out it is a symptom of unproductive conditions, i.e. the air temperature being far too low in comparison with that of the water. It follows by contrast that low cloud or mist, descending from above so to speak, and not arising from the river is not necessarily harmful, and it is worth continuing fishing even in a fog if the air is warmer or at least no colder than the water. I have seen many fish caught in such circumstances, though I think most fishermen would take a poor view of them.

A uniformly cloudy sky with a subdued light, what is sometimes termed a 'grey' day, provides what is perhaps not the most auspicious light for fishing, particularly in cold weather. Nevertheless it is much better than glaring summer sunshine, and the angler should in no way be discouraged by it. A 'leaden' sky, as it is sometimes described, is on the other hand often a precursor of thunder, and if so is definitely a drawback. Prior to a thunder-storm, when the air is overcharged with electricity, fish seldom if ever take, and they are better then left in peace.

To sum up therefore as to the best sort of light for fishing, one could say that a day of clear clean atmosphere, with a certain number of cumulus clouds veiling at intervals a reasonably bright though not too strong sun, provides a good prospect, but during hot summer weather a subdued light, particularly that of the early morning, is best.

One sort of light has not yet been touched upon, and that is moonlight! Whether salmon can be caught by moonlight or not I do not know. Mr Neville Bostock, an expert angler of the early years of this century says definitely that they can (see Anthony Crossley's *Floating Line for Salmon and Sea Trout*, page 127). On the other hand it seems to be a universal axiom amongst sea-trout fishers that a bright moon spells frustration.

So what may be the truth about salmon taking in moonlight is uncertain. It might on some occasion or other be quite interesting to experiment in this matter, but I feel it should be left at that. Would not the large majority of my fellow anglers agree that at such times when the moon is bright the fish should be left in peace? Angling on most rivers is already far too intensive, and is not dawn to dusk long enough for it? Think of the horror if moonlight fishing by any chance was found to be effective, so that anglers felt in duty bound to continue all round the clock at time of clear moonlight nights.

III

ANGLING AND RIVERCRAFT

The mist is lifting, and conditions will soon be good

6

Types of River

When and where he is going to fish are two considerations to which the salmon angler would be well advised to give close attention. There are many widely varying types of salmon river, which in turn only fish well at certain different times of year.

Obviously therefore anyone who is planning to fish somewhere previously unknown to him should take the trouble to find out exactly what type of river he is proposing to visit, whether it fulfills his idea of the sort of fishing he likes, and whether it fishes well at the time of year when he is going there.

This may seem platitudinous, but it is surprising how many people every season fail to do exactly the above, and then complain later that they have been led astray! All rivers are different, and need fishing at different periods of the season, and with different tactics, if the best is to be made of them.

Of course if you are a 'small river man', and you are taken to fish the Tay or the Spey in early spring, for example, you will probably be disillusioned. Equally someone used through all his fishing career to the Tweed, Wye, or Ness, will most probably find the Grimersta, Gruinard, or Dart pretty trivial. Equally, if owing to advancing years or lameness or something of this sort you are reluctant to wade deep, it is no good going to a river like the Dee, Ness, or Lochy. The Naver, Helmsdale, Oykel, Stinchar, or some smaller river of that size should be your choice.

Time of year also is an important factor. Certain rivers fish best in spring, notably the Aberdeenshire Dee. Others have their best run of fish from July onwards, more and more of them in these present days, for instance the Naver, Helmsdale, Oykel, Ness, Spey, Lochy and Awe, to name but a few of them. The Tweed and Nith on the other hand now fish best in autumn, right on into November. It follows that it is of very little use trying to catch salmon in these and similar rivers at other times than during their good fishing period, or that if you attempt to do so you must do it with your eyes open, not being disappointed if your bag is light or even empty.

What is more, in addition to going to the right river at the right time, you should try and go to the right part of it. For instance, it would be preferable to delay fishing the Spey in its upper reaches until after the second week in April, as normally before this period the fishing affords less chance of success. The same could be said of the upper Dee in the Ballater area and above. Similarly to fish on the lower Dee below Aboyne in June or thereafter is also likely to lead to disappointment (except it should be noted that the Dee in years long ago was a good autumn river, and is beginning to show signs of tending that way again). By June in normal circumstances the main stock of fish should be reckoned to be well through the bottom half of the Dee. This point seems so obvious that it should need no elaboration. Yet every season one sees and hears of good beats being let either too early or too late in the season; it is to be hoped that the tenants at such times will be paying a lower rent to compensate for the poorer chances. It is important to remember that no beat, however good, can possibly fish really well throughout the legal fishing season. None ever has, and none ever will.

Turning now to different types and different sizes of river, here we find a kaleidoscope of varieties. Do you like really large rivers which are boat fished, and where wading is at a discount? If so, something like the Rauma, Evanger, lower Tay, lower Tweed, or parts of the lower Spey might be your choice. The advantages of such large rivers are many. They provide the chance of really big fish of anywhere between 30lb. and 50lb., or even larger, as well as of plenty of smaller ones. Playing fish of this large size in a big river is an immense thrill, and such leviathans are often lost which only adds to the drama. There is plenty of room on such rivers for the most ambitious fisherman to open his shoulders and throw his longest possible line, and less chance of interference from or to other anglers. Casting from a boat should be the normal method of fishing (I am by-passing harling as being a second rate activity) and this may be a relief from wading if the stream is fast or deep. Nevertheless there are likely to be odd 'neuks' or shallower stretches where wading as an alternative can be adopted, if so wanted. Another advantage of large rivers is that they never fall low enough to stop fish running, provided they get past the nets. Indeed many of them, the Tay for example, fish best with the water on the low side.

Naturally they have their attendant drawbacks. If the angler, owing to absence of boat or boatman, *has* to wade, this is likely to be hard work. It will probably involve entering deep into a strong stream, and will be hazardous for anyone other than an accomplished performer. It is important that the angler should be capable of throwing a long line, even from a boat, let alone when wading. Short casts of twenty to twenty-four yards or so are of little use on rivers of this type. Thirty to thirty-five yards is much more to the point. Casting such a line, or any line for that matter, may be difficult and tiring in a high wind, and big rivers are apt to be less sheltered than small ones. Playing large and active fish, when they have a strong current to help them and unlimited room to run, can be a difficult process as well as exhausting (though perhaps this should be accounted an advantage rather than a drawback!). Finally big rivers do have one substantial disadvantage, they seldom fish well when in flood; and flood they do, after any quantity of rain or melting snow, sometimes taking several days to run down and clear into reasonable fishing order. Nevertheless rivers of this size probably provide a fairer chance of being in good fishing order for a longer period of time than any others.

Medium sized rivers have different characteristics, though in some ways they are similar. I have in mind the Lochy, Awe, Deveron, Beauly, Findhorn, and others of similar type and size. Although big fish from rivers such as these are now rare, their capture still occurs occasionally (as lately as last season, 1982, a fish of 40lb. was taken from the Spean, a tributary of the Lochy). Such rivers do not demand such deep wading, nor do they require such a long line, in fact it boils down to their being 'easier' to fish. All the same there is room in them for an active fish to run out a long line and give plenty of excitement in play, and there is also room for an enterprising angler to exercise his skill in throwing a good length of line from time to time. Boats become unnecessary, which must please those who prefer wading, and floods when they occur are limited both in duration and resulting damage.

On the other hand, medium sized rivers in time of continued fine weather can fall too low for fish to run; one is then left with the old potted residents of long standing, which have become uncatchable, while any fresh ones entering the estuary are caught in nets. This is the main drawback where such rivers are concerned, and it can be a disheartening one with no possibility of being foreseen any distance ahead.

Small rivers present a very different problem. The angler is largely dependent on enough rain falling from time to time to put the river into 'fishing order' and preferably to keep it there as long as possible. High floods are welcome, and it is the prolonged drought of long periods of fine rainless weather with the river down to low summer level which brings fishing to a standstill. Rivers of this type might include the Naver, Helmsdale, Stinchar, Oykel, Dart and Tamar. Such rivers are 'easier' to fish in that fishing them demands less hard work, though more finesse. It is an advantage for the fisher to know the water like the back of his hand, to a yard where fish are likely to be lying, and where are the best taking places. No deep wading will be necessary, and in fact if wading is needed at all thigh waders will be fully adequate. Except in time of spate, a single handed rod and a short line may be all that is needed; 12 to 14 feet will in any case be the maximum length required. There will most probably be a great number of small pools and a great variety of them at the anglers disposal, and it will most likely not take more than ten minutes to fish each one of them if no fish responds. Such is the continually changing charm of small rivers, and a skilled technique is required in fishing them if fish are to be caught in numbers. Even two or three salmon or grilse taken in one day may constitute a praisworthy effort.

On the other hand small river fish are likely in turn to run small. A 20lb. salmon will be outsized, and the average will probably be down to 7lb. or so. There will be no room for a long line to be thrown, which indeed will never be needed . . . And there will usually be little excitement in playing fish, which if considered a derogatory statement is confirmed by the fact that small fish seldom put up a prolonged or determined fight even in a big river, let alone a small one.

So all types of river have their merits and drawbacks; and before he undertakes to fish any one of them I suggest the angler thinks over all the above points carefully before he reaches a firm decision. Everyone is apt to have differing views on this subject. Personally, if the preference of an individual is of any guidance, I like all types of salmon river from the largest to the smallest, but at the same time I would not care to be bound to any single one for any great length of time. Is not variety the spice of life? and I for one so much enjoy the different problems and different techniques that apply on a wide diversity of waters.

If I was pressed closely to define my ideal salmon river, I would find it difficult to give a concise answer, realizing at the same time that what suits one person best does not necessarily suit another. However my own choice might be governed as follows:

(a) It would be a river where there was a fair chance of a 40 pounder upwards.

(b) There would also have to be a fair number of smaller fish available, though not necessarily a vast quantity of them.

(c) There would have to be a strong current in the river, with plenty of well defined and varying pools, and a rocky and gravelly bed, thus providing interesting fishing, and making the play of the fish exciting.

(d) It would have to be a river which could be covered by casting from a boat or by wading (or both). A harling river would be of no interest.

(e) There would have to be pleasant and peaceful surroundings, preferably hilly or mountainous.

(f) The water in its normal state would have to run clear, the clearer the better, though allowed to colour in flood.

(g) There would have to be reasonable accommodation available (though not necessarily luxurious) and fairly close at hand.

(h) Above all the fishing would have to be reasonably extensive, with plenty of elbow room so that rods did not tread on each others toes, and the river would have to be of a fair size.

Does this sound to the reader something on the lines of a good Norwegian river? Perhaps he would not be far out if he chose to regard it so.

7
Reading a River

The ability by limited scrutiny of a river to form a reasonably accurate estimate of where fish are likely to be lying, and where they will take, is a valuable one.

'Reading a river' is, I think, a trans-Atlantic expression, which most fishermen would assume implied primarily the above ability, coupled with being able to make a reasonable assessment of how its salmon in general will behave, judging by its appearance. Also it implies being able to evaluate the character of the river itself, and how it in turn is likely to behave at different seasons and under different weather conditions.

No two salmon rivers are quite the same, and some, so far as British rivers are concerned, differ immensely. Compare, for instance, the large and turbulent Spey with the slow and circuitous Frome—what a total contrast! And yet both are salmon rivers, producing fish similar in size, if not in numbers. Compare too a huge and rapid waterway such as the Norwegian Namsen with the tiny five yards wide Little River on the Test at Nursling. Again both are salmon rivers, but they have little else in common.

Obviously there can be no overall rules of guidance in 'reading' such a wide variety of rivers. What is certain, however, is that anyone who knows one section of a particular river well, will be able to evaluate pretty accurately the character of any other section of that same river. He will also be able to do the same, though perhaps with slightly less certainty, in the case of any other similar river in the neighbourhood. For instance, an angler well acquainted with the Dee near Banchory will also be at home with it in the Ballater area. He is also likely to be able to 'read' adequately neighbouring rivers such as the Deveron, North Esk and South Esk. The Spey and the Tay are larger, and could be put in a different category to the Dee; but a Spey expert would be able to read the Tay adequately and vice versa. There is sufficient resemblance.

A Scottish fisherman up to a point would be at home on Icelandic or Norwegian rivers, though to a lesser degree. There are usually certain marked differences the wider apart the rivers in question lie. And inevitably one is inclined to group rivers into categories, fast or slow, rocky or silty, big, medium, or small, mountain torrents or lowland waterways, with fishing by boat, wading, or from the bank, and so on—the varieties are endless, and all these variations where the successful 'reading' of a river is concerned have to be taken into consideration.

One type of feature is common on most rivers and its effects everywhere similar, that is obstructions to the passage of fish. These may take varying forms, such as natural falls, weirs, caulds, dykes, mill hatches, or in Norway, heavy and prolonged rapids. Even ill-designed and inefficient fish passes can be grouped in this category, when the fish congregate in numbers below them, reluctant to attempt the ascent.

As long as the water is cold, say at 42°F or less, salmon are unwilling to exert themselves in surmounting any sizeable obstacle, so at these temperatures they should be looked for downstream of it. The falls at Kildonan on the Helmsdale, or at the head of the Darnaway water on the Findhorn, or the dyke at Kinnaird on the South Esk are examples of this. Fish may lie for any distance downstream of such obstructions, how far down depending on the size of their shoals.

An interesting point should be noticed here. On occasions where there is an obstacle such as a weir or fall which temporarily checks their passage, fish may be found spread out in the river below it for a considerable distance downstream, perhaps for half a mile or more. It might be thought that if the ascent of fish through the obstruction is then made easier by new ladders, or partial removal, or something similar, that the fish that lay at a distance downstream would not be affected, i.e. that the ones lying right below the obstruction or in its immediate neighbourhood might be expected to pass quickly upstream, though those in the habit of lying a quarter to half a mile downstream would continue to halt there and not be affected at so long a range. But make no mistake, this does not happen! If the leaders in the queue are allowed to pass on readily, the laggards will follow them; and the whole situation in regard to whether or not a stretch of fishing continues to hold fish in numbers may be largely changed by the easing or elimination of obstructions. I have seen this happen more than once. A rough parallel may be seen at the platform gates at, say, Waterloo Station. As long as the gates are closed, or virtually so, the queue of passengers forms, and latecomers attach themselves to its tail. But when the gates are opened the whole queue steadily passes through—not that this happens so drastically in the case of salmon, as it is assumed that odd fish will continually ascend the obstruction even in cold water, and that as the temperature warms still a certain number will remain downstream for a period of time, even though the majority pass upstream. But the overall effect is similar.

To return to the general picture, where there is an obstruction of this sort, on any type of river, the first place an angler should look for fish is in suitable lies for some distance downstream of it. The second place is not quite so obvious, it is immediately upstream of it. The reason is that, once fish have started to ascend an obstacle in numbers, some of them are almost certain to stop to rest from their exertions a short distance upstream, rather in the manner of an alpine climber resting in a mountain hut halfway up a difficult ascent. The pool known as the Putt above Kelso cauld on the Tweed is a noteworthy example of this, as are numerous stretches on the Test and Avon immediately upstream of hatches; in fact there are many such examples on many different rivers.

Returning to general procedure in 'reading' a river, on arrival on a strange water the angler's first glance at it should take in its size and speed of flow. If it is a north-country river it is likely to be gravelly, rocky and fast running, with clear cut rapids, pools and flats; there are exceptions of course, the lower Tweed and the lower Don for instance, but the above is the character of most of them.

Where fish are likely to be lying in such a river depends on time of year, resultant water temperature and height, and strength of current. In early spring and late autumn the water is likely to be cold, perhaps at 42°F or less. As already noted in chapter three, fish at this temperature like to lie in the slacker and deeper water, such as is found in the middle section of pools. They are unlikely to seek fast and shallow streams. If the water is high, and there is enough depth there, they may be found close under the bank; so the river height is another factor which should be ascertained at once. If the beat is unknown it may be difficult to estimate its height straightaway, but high water marks along the bank, coupled with general speed of flow, also with the clarity or otherwise of the water, and debris or absence of it on the surface, should give a fairly accurate indication.

The next thing to be established is whether the water is steady, falling, or rising, a vital consideration. The state of the weather should give a preliminary indication of this. If there has been no rain lately it is not likely to be rising (though high wind on a headwater loch or the operations of a Hydro could have this effect). In any case any tendency to rise is easily spotted by the surface tension causing a bulge on the water edge, as the water creeps up on stones. With rising water one naturally expects some if not all the fish to be on the move, and one looks for them in such places as described in chapter four on Water Height.

With the water steady or falling after a few days fine weather (and these conditions should be easily confirmed from an examination of high water marks on the bank, coupled with observation of water level on stones barely showing above the surface), fish will be lying in the more orthodox places. With the water cold they will certainly prefer deep slack water as described above. As it gets warmer they will move more and more into the shallower streamy water, particularly where the bottom is broken so as to give them shelter from the current. This is where one should then look for them, and these are also likely to be the best taking places. The tail of a pool is usually a good holding place, given the right depth and speed of water. It is helped if there are sizeable boulders on the bottom situated in the normal 'run' of the fish, which can give shelter. Such places are likely to form especially good temporary lies for running fish, which may pause there on first entering the pool.

A selection of salmon flies in present day use

As to depth, the best indication which can be given is that fish, as I have said earlier, prefer water from around 4 feet in depth to 8 feet, and that is where one should look for them. They do also like deep water below their lie, where they can take refuge if alarmed, though this is not always available. They will lie shallower if the water is warm, and deeper if it is cold.

Boils, not too large, on the surface are a certain indication of sunken boulders or outcrops of rock. These often provide good lies for fish, if the depth is reasonable, by breaking the current, and so giving shelter. Special attention when fishing should be given to them; and it should be remembered that fish are just as likely to lie upstream of them as well as to one side of them or well below them.

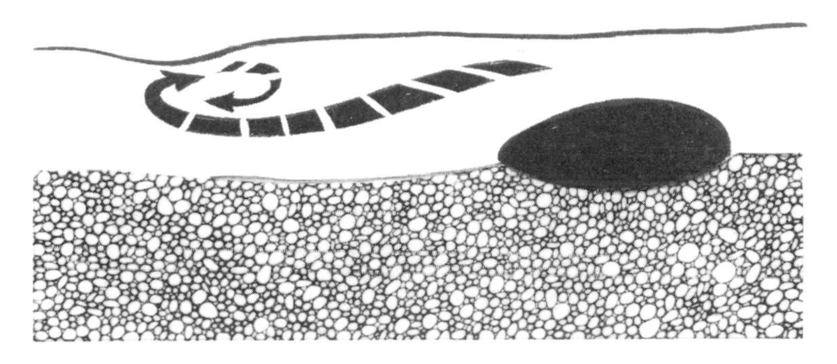

The problem for the fisherman is to estimate the position of the boulder, and cover the surrounding water adequately.

The boil itself in any case is likely to appear some distance downstream of the boulder that causes it, depending on the speed of the current. It should be made clear that the term 'boils' here refers to individual and comparatively small up-wellings in the water, such as are created by an individual stone or boulder. Big areas of boiling and eddying water are quite another matter, and fish normally dislike and avoid them. In big rivers such as the Spey and Tay such large areas of boiling water or 'whirly holes' occur not infrequently, but it is a waste of time looking for salmon in them. They prefer a steady, direct, and reasonably brisk current, undiverted into different directions; and if such a current is too strong for them they will lie where the stream slackens on either side of it.

The list of such appreciations may seem long drawn-out on paper, but on the river the experienced fisherman should make them in a matter of minutes, if not seconds, and they should be made almost automatically. There is little difficulty in discovering what one wants to know if one knows where to look for it and how to find it.

Jumping fish are another feature which should be taken into consideration (see chapter one). If fresh fish are seen jumping continuously in the same place it is a sure indication that they are lying there. (The only possible exception to this could be at some impossible lie such as the shallow head of a rapid, where successive running fish are apt to show as they pass through it on their way upstream.)

The jump of kelts is also worth watching. Sometimes kelts both lie and jump in places where fresh fish could never be found, e.g. in very shallow or very slack water. Such jumps should be disregarded. But if a kelt jumps in any place which appears a likely lie for fresh fish this lie should be noted and fished, as kelts and fresh fish often lie in company together; more than one good salmon could be thus located. If running fish are seen jumping, and obviously passing through in numbers, the angler should hasten upstream to wherever is the next sizeable obstruction in the way of fall, weir, or strong rapid. It is likely that some members of the shoal will stop there long enough to be caught, if the water is not rising (or perhaps even if it is).

So far I have written about rivers in high or normal conditions, but without mention of summer levels or below. As the river gets very low as well as warm, fish being worried about their security will naturally fall back into the deeper holes—preferably with a slight stream through them. These will be their main refuge, and where they may be expected. As dusk falls, or in early morning, they may work their way into the shallow streams presumably in search of more oxygenated water; but they will probably find such streams too shallow for their liking when the sun is well up, and will drop back again to the deeper places.

Little mention has so far been made of colour in the water. This affects the lie of fish little if at all, but it does affect their taking, which is outside the scope of this chapter. One point worth noticing, however, which I learnt on the Spey, is this—when the water is peated after a spate, so that fish are sickened, the best place to fish is on any gravel flats where fish may be lying. The shallow or 'thin' water is best, provided there are fish in it, and I have seen it pay on many occasions to fish a coloured river in such places. If, therefore, you can 'read' a coloured river sufficiently accurately to discover the whereabouts of gravel flats, where odd fish are jumping from time to time (which surely is not too difficult?), it may well bring you success.

I have referred mainly in this chapter to the faster north-country rivers which indeed carry the main salmon stocks of Britain. Slow running south-country rivers, such as the Test, Avon and Frome fall into quite another category. They are much more difficult to 'read' and their stock of fish is less extensive. One never there finds a pool holding fish in scores or fifties, as one often does further north. It is a question of the odd fish here and there, and until one knows the river well it may be a difficult question finding them. These rivers look very similar throughout their course.

A hatch or weir, as with obstructions elsewhere,

usually provides a lie either upstream or downstream (or both). In a hatch pool the main rush from the hatch downwards is usually non-productive—fish are sometimes found in the tail of it, it is true, where the current slows up, but where above all they like to lie is in the back-run on either side, where the water swings back again, upstream so to speak, close to the bank, and back towards the hatch.

Elsewhere in these south-country rivers fish prefer a moderate depth of water, and a steady and direct flow of medium strength. They like outcrops on the bottom, the whereabouts of which are advertised by boils on the surface, and they like too the neck and tail of deep holes. Weed growth, in moderation, attracts rather than repels. They often like to lie tight under the bank, if the depth and strength of water are suitable. They do not like water full of big boils and eddies, nor water either choked by weed or bare of it. A pronounced bend in the river's course usually leads to the formation of a good lie, either right on the bend or immediately above it or below. This last is a characteristic in the case of north-country rivers as well.

How admirable it would be if one could only go down to a strange river, and say with certainty: 'There's where a fish is lying, and there! and there! And by that rock there must be a certain holding place!', and so on. Unfortunately one can't, not with certainty, and the best-looking holding places sometimes turn out to be wholly unproductive. However, one can at least aim at probabilities, and as experience increases, the probabilities are likely to come closer to certainties.

One further point which should always be borne in mind is that, after every big flood, the river bottom and consequently the salmon lies, are liable to change. Some remain unaltered, but new ones are liable to come, and old ones to go. After such a flood therefore the fisherman should lose no time in making a fresh diagnosis of his beat. If the water falls low, it may be useful to travel the length of it in a boat to make a closer inspection of the bottom.

In conclusion, I would emphasize again that the best guide to any unknown part of a river is the thorough knowledge of some other part of that same river—that is always of course in default of the guidance of some local expert, if he is kind enough to give his services—(much time is saved thereby).

8
Casting

As this subject has been so exhaustively described and discussed in many other books, this chapter will be brief. I am sure that my readers are already proficient casters, this being the first activity that one undertakes when learning to fish.

Although casting is only the initial stage in the process of fishing, it is nevertheless an important one. No bad caster was ever a successful fisherman. One should never be satisfied with one's casting performance, and should always be attempting to improve it in any way possible.

Bait casting is a comparatively simple process with the various modern types of 'easicast' reel (very different from the old Nottingham or Silex). What is more, it can be as effectively practised as regards distance and accuracy on the lawn as on the water. With a suitable outfit its accomplishment up to an effective standard presents little difficulty.

Fly casting is another matter, and takes longer to learn well. Much depends on using a suitable rod with a line of appropriate weight. For small rivers single handed casting with a rod of up to 10 feet in length is useful in low water, though in spate double handed with a rod of up to 13 feet may be better. On medium sized rivers, such as the Lochy, Dee, Awe, Deveron, and so on, most anglers prefer a double handed rod of between 11 feet and 14 feet. Only a high wind or big water may create a need for something longer. On big rivers, like the Spey or Tay, 14 feet is the minimum useful length, and in Norway longer still.

The advent of carbon-graphite as a rod material has revolutionized the situation as regards long rods. A 17 foot carbon-graphite rod weighs less than a 14 foot split-cane, so there is absolutely no reason nowadays for rejecting a long carbon rod of say sixteen, seventeen, or even eighteen feet on the grounds of weight.

The longer the rod (provided it has an effective action and is used with a line of the right weight), the longer the cast that can comfortably be made; and on a big river or even a medium one the ability to throw a long line whenever wanted is invaluable. Thirty-five yards is none too long a distance to be aimed at, as I have previously said.

Most fishermen however still use rods of a maximum length of 14 feet, which makes a cast of this distance impossible. They handicap themselves on any sizeable river by so doing.

The overhead cast is the normal method employed by the vast majority of fly fishermen. This cast is adequate for small rivers where accuracy is the main objective. It is less effective on medium and large rivers, particularly when a long line is needed. A variety of drawbacks attend it, e.g. any obstruction behind the angler can make this cast impossible, flies are cracked off, and hooks get broken on stones behind or hooked in grass or bushes, wind knots are often formed in the leader, and so on.

The Spey cast in contrast is far more effective. If the right outfit is used a good Spey caster will put yards onto the overhead man's throw. Obstructions behind the caster are no obstacle, e.g. the angler can cast a full throw standing at the foot of a rock face or with trees and bushes behind him. Wind knots become infrequent, flies are not flicked off, nor are hook points broken. Direction of wind makes little difference, if the double Spey is used when it is downstream. Only a strong wind blowing from more or less directly across the river can make things awkward; and only if the bank is overgrown right down to the water's edge is the fly liable to be hung up from time to time. Otherwise the Spey cast could fairly be described as having no disadvantages, in fact very much the contrary for both short or long casts. Personally I have now for a number of years pretty well foresaken the overhead cast, except in exceptional circumstances, as being by comparison both clumsy and inefficient.

If the reader is already fortunate enough to be a skilled performer of the Spey cast, I am confident he will endorse all the above remarks. But if he is not, he may well ask how to learn this cast. Unfortunately he will find instructions from books virtually useless. One has seen numbers of illustrations, with fishermen sometimes wearing bowler hats, and rods and lines weaving a series of complicated and intricate paths through the air! Such diagrams are more or less unintelligible, until one can already Spey cast reasonably well, when they begin to make some sense (though a bit late in the day). No, tuition by an expert on the river is the only answer. Such a tutor, unfortunately, will be difficult to find except on the Spey, Ness, Findhorn, or perhaps the Dee. It is a waste of time trying to learn this cast on a lawn, and little better on still water. The pull of a flowing current is what is wanted. In addition there is even more need than with the overhead cast to be fully ambidextrous. The double Spey must also be learnt, but few people find this difficult once the single

Spey has been mastered.

This all sounds rather difficult and complicated, nevertheless with the right tackle and good tuition I can assure the reader that it is not so. I do recommend him to lose no opportunity of learning this cast, preferably at as early an age as possible, (that is if he is not already expert at it). If he can find a good instructor, and thus become proficient, I know he will never regret either the trouble or expense.

* * *

I said earlier that much depends on using a suitable rod with the right weight of line. As an afterthought this makes one wonder how our grandfathers, who considered 18 feet the proper length of a salmon rod, stood up to the strain of using those very heavy rods over long periods of fishing.

The author, thanks to the kindness of Major J. Godman of Ness Side, once had the opportunity of handling spliced greenheart rods of 18 feet and longer which formerly belonged to Alexander Grant, the great switch caster of Victorian times, made famous in Jock Scott's book *Fine and Far Off*. Although they would doubtless throw an immense length of line, these rods seemed unbelievably cumbersome—back breaking on a long day's fishing one would have thought, and yet Grant was said to have been a small man! On the other hand a 12 bore shot gun which one handles throughout a day's shooting is much heavier. Why therefore does an old fashioned 18 foot rod seem so cumbersome? I think it is partly due to the marked contrast between the old and the new; on the one hand the old fashioned wooden rod, of heavy greenheart, with its brass rings and fittings, and on the other the modern ultra-light rod of carbon graphite with light metal fittings. The difference in respective weights is outstanding. But if one wonders how the anglers of the past managed to cope with such (to our mind) unwieldy implements, the answer would seem to lie under the heading of 'balance'. One handles a much heavier shot gun without inconvenience all day because one holds and carries it in such a way as to make use of its 'balance'. As a result of proper handling a well-balanced gun does not seem too heavy, even on a day when one fires off from it several hundred cartridges. This is because during most of the time it is held or supported at the 'point of balance'.

In a similar way there was an art in wielding the old

fashioned long and heavy rods, which today has largely been lost. The most important feature was that the base of the rod with its rubber button should on no account be held into the stomach while the cast was being fished round, as is the normal custom with the modern much lighter rod. Invariably after the forward cast had been completed the rod was held at the point of balance, which was somewhere near the top of the cork hand grip, and the butt of the rod was allowed to extend behind the angler. In this way all strain on the back muscles during the process of fishing was avoided, and the rod handled in this way seemed lighter. This made an immense difference to fatigue or otherwise at the end of a long day's fishing.

The second important piece of advice given by all the experts of the time was 'to let the rod do the work'—that is to say not to use stress or force when casting, (one is reminded of being told 'not to press' in golf), but to rely on rhythm and timing coupled with the innate power of the rod's action when harnessed to a line of suitable weight (the latter also being an important factor).

Avoidance of strain, avoidance of stress, in these two phrases therefore must lie the secret of the way in which their old fashioned rods were successfully wielded. No doubt in skilled hands they threw an excellent line, but the art of handling them without strain was none too easy to acquire. Fortunately, perhaps, such an art is no longer so vital a requirement for the modern angler. To digress for a moment, the length of these old fashioned rods is often derided, and one hears sarcastic witticisms attributed to the anglers of the day on the lines of: 'It is not true that 20 foot rods are essential. Quite often 19 feet is long enough', and so on. But in fact the original reason for the greath length of these rods was a sound one. The waterproof oil-dressed silk flyline was only invented in the mid-1850s and was not in general use until later. In the early years of the century lines were made of plaited silk or horse-hair, or a mixture of the two, very light and difficult to cast to any distance, particularly against an adverse wind. It was quite natural therefore that salmon rods should be of what we would consider exorbitant length. Such rods helped enormously with lines of this type to cover any fish lying at more than say 18 yards distance.

Fishermen are by nature a conservative race, and even with the advent of the easily cast and heavier oil dressed silk line it was long before they realized that shorter lengths for a salmon rod rather than the standard 18 feet could be valuable. Trout rods under the same circumstances went through a similar though delayed reduction in length.

By way of comparison, 30 inches was once the standard length for a shot gun barrel, dating back to the days of black powder and muzzle loaders. Every objection was originally put forward to any shortening of this standard length, and it was only after a considerable passage of time that 28 inch barrels were adopted, and even 26 inch, by many shooting enthusiasts. The old order in shooting, as in fishing, is apt to die hard.

9

Controlling the Water-Speed of the Fly

Much has been said and written about the size and colour of salmon flies, their construction, appearance, and the materials of which they are made. There is one factor about them, however, to which it seems to me far too little attention has been paid, and that is their water-speed while they are being fished.

This is perhaps a more important consideration than any of the other features listed above.

The fisherman takes great trouble, or should do, to impart to his fly when fishing the appearance of life. He casts it diagonally across the current so that it 'swims' across the lie of the fish. When it reaches slow water towards the end of the cast, he pulls in line (to be shot with the next throw) thus making the fly travel upstream through the water. But I wonder how many fishermen are really giving thought to the motion of their fly in the fish's eyes when they are doing this, as opposed to blindly following the traditional well-worn path?

We know that a salmon will rarely interest himself in an object that appears completely dead in the water, lacking all life. It is true that he will occasionally take a dry fly floating down without drag, or a nymph-like lure carried down by the current again without drag. But does not his attention in these cases usually have to be aroused by anything up to a hundred or more repeated casts if necessary? And does not the continual reappearance of such lures give an illusion of life, coupled with the slight movement of their feathers and hackle points. And do not most dry fly experts tell us that a certain amount of drag, giving a semblance of life, is desirable? In the words of G. L. Ashley-Dodd in *A Fisherman's Log*: 'When a dragged fly goes over a salmon, up he comes!'

Most of us at one time or another have seen a salmon snatch at a piece of thistledown blown across the surface of the water. Here is an illustration of the attraction of lifelike motion. The thistledown floating downstream unmoved by wind would be unlikely to attract; yet when blown across the river it must give an impression of some creature scurrying in a lifelike yet unusual way across the water, and so attracts the salmon's predatory instinct. Is not this motion approaching very closely to that of a hackled dry-fly dragged?

Lifelike motion in a downstream sunken or sub-surface fly is even more important. If the reader asks what is my authority for this rather arbitrary statement, I can only answer 'experience' coupled with observation of the reaction of salmon to my friends' flies when fished in different ways and to my own. One should never be afraid to experiment when fishing; one learns so much by doing so, as well as by watching others doing it. If one can actually see the salmon in the water when one is fishing for him, as is often possible in Iceland where I fished for 18 years, one learns more in an hour than in years of fishing 'blindly'.

Perhaps I can best approach this subject by pointing out that there are many fishermen who think that once they have cast a fair line across the water, and if their fly does not 'skate' or otherwise misbehave, they have done all that is required for the time being. They reckon that it is now the business of the current to carry their line round, until it has straightened out below them. They then pull in a yard or two of line, take a step or two down, and repeat the process till a fish takes or till they reach the bottom of the pool. If there is not enough stream to carry the fly round, they write off the pool as being 'too low to fish', and move off elsewhere. They will sometimes catch fish in this way without doubt, and if there are plenty of good takers in the pools they may catch quite a number. Nevertheless the intelligent fisherman who uses his imagination, and can transmit his will-power to the passage of his fly through the water, as opposed to simply letting the current do it for him (if it will), will catch two or three times as many fish.

It should be realized that in the fish's mind the downstream fished fly appears as a small creature swimming on its own initiative against or across the stream, not as something held in the stream by a leader or line in the way it appears to the angler. Above all this creature must not appear to the fish to swim unnaturally fast, and must avoid being apparently possessed of uncanny or unnatural power enabling it to do so. For example if the current is a fast one, say of 6 knots, a fly hanging (to human eyes) motionless in this current in the fish's eyes is swimming at 6 knots merely in order to hold its position! It is extremely unlikely that a natural creature as small as a fly of around size 6 could achieve this. It certainly could not maintain a greater water-speed, so if in addition the angler pulls in line and makes the fly move upstream, the effect from being most probably unnatural becomes most certainly so. And the salmon will not take it. On the other hand if the fly is say three and a half inches long, it is more likely and perhaps just possible that a creature of this increased size could hold its own against such a current. The salmon sees what he imagines is a small creature just able to swim with the greatest difficulty against a strong stream; but it is not unnatural, it does not repel him, in fact it arouses his predatory instinct, and his reaction may be to take it. Here is the background behind the fact that large flies in strong streams are much more effective than small ones. It is a question of the water-speed of the fly in relation to its size. And the other factor is of course that for a salmon to leave his lie in a strong stream and chase after a fly or bait involves considerable effort; he is not likely to expend such effort in pursuit of something insignificant. On the other hand he may well think differently about a prey of considerable size, well worth catching. Is not the angler's attitude similar, when he shuns wading into a very rough strong stream in pursuit of petty herling or grilse, but will breast a formidable torrent if he sees a 40 pounder jump where by so wading he can cover it?

Consider too the effect on fish of large flies in *slack* water. They must be kept moving to attract. Hanging motionless they seldom if ever are taken. If the water is very cold in spring or autumn it is true that only slight motion is required, but as it approaches normal temperatures the fly should be moved faster and faster in proportion to its size. I have seen salmon and grilse in a loch frequently caught on three inch flies trolled at 4 knots through the still water when they would not look at the small conventional sizes either trolled or cast—not that I advocate trolling, but it affords an interesting sidelight on the subject of fly size in relation to water speed. The same effect is given by stripping a fly fast through slack water, or by 'backing up' either on foot or with a boat.

Conversely the smaller the size of fly the less movement through the water is necessary. Very tiny Stoats Tails or Black Pennells on fine gut require little motion while being fished.

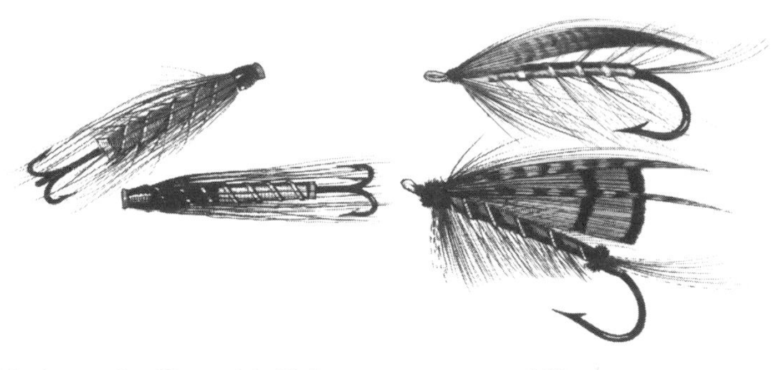

Modern tube flies with 19th century gut-eyed flies

To sum up, the fisherman should at all times be in complete control of both the speed and passage of his fly as it travels through the water; he should not simply rely on the stream to fish his fly for him, but should be conscious all the time of the necessary speed at which the fly should be fished in relation both to its size and the strength of the current, which may vary from turbulent in mid-stream to sluggish nearer the bank. If he can achieve such control and vary it as seems good both to him and the fish, he will find both interest and catch greatly increased.

It may well be asked at this stage how such control

is to be achieved? Most fishermen already know of A. H. E. Wood's method of controlling the speed at which his fly travelled across the stream, fast or slow or hanging steady as required. It was by 'mending' his greased line one way or the other, as needed. This was all very well, and it doubtless proved highly successful on the well stocked waters of the clear, shallow, and streamy Aberdeenshire Dee. But its effective scope was limited. What if there was little or no stream to make the fly 'swim', or to carry it round? Or if the fish were lying deep in slow and solid pools, such as are sometimes found on the Wye, Tweed, Cork Blackwater, lower Spey, or Tay? The use of small flies, fished slowly and near the surface in Wood's Cairnton style, is not good enough for pools like these; and it also is apt to fall short in many pools on small rivers when the water drops to summer level.

It is true that Wood's method at times is of great use, for example where there is a *strong* current close to the near bank, easing off into slacker water beyond where the fish lie. Instances of pools of this type are the Boat Pool at Easter Elchies and Creichie at Aikenway, both on the Spey. The angler needs to make a long throw across the stream in such places, followed by a powerful upstream 'mend' (or even two of them), to slow up the passage of the fly so that the current does not whip it round too fast. Equally a downstream 'mend' at other times can be useful, to make the fly move at an increased and more attractive speed through a piece of slack water where fish are lying.

But what Wood's method seems to lack is the essential ability to exercise full control of the water-speed of the fly. He left it too much to the current to fish the fly, in the place of the angler. The water-speed of the fly should be governed, partly by Wood's method of 'mending' it is true, but far more so by the stripping of line by hand through the rod rings at whatever speed may be required. In this way the fly can be made to fish attractively through water travelling at any speed from fast and rapid to slow and stagnant. In fast water for instance no stripping need be done, the current by itself imparting water-speed to the fly, until the fly reaches slacker water at the edge of the stream and the line has straightened out below. Several yards of line should then be stripped at an appropriate speed so as to make the fly move at an attractive pace through the water . . . not too fast so as to make it appear unnatural in the fish's eyes, but enough to give it life and give the fish the idea that it is trying to escape from him. The line thus drawn in can be 'shot' with the next cast, or after a preliminary false cast if its length is excessive.

As the stream becomes slacker towards the middle or tail of a pool, so the water-speed of the fly should be increased in this fashion. If a fish moves at the fly, but does not touch it, he can be tried again with the fly being made to move faster or slower as seems best. This method of fly-control can be used in all speeds of current, from rapid to stagnant, and can be made to raise fish in all of them.

There are two attendant though minor difficulties. One is the constant shooting of a long length of slack line, probably five yards or more, when the cast is made; but with practice, and with the use of modern plastic coated lines that shoot so freely, this soon becomes easier. It is surprising how long a line eventually *can* be shot. The other is how to hook and handle a fish which takes when several yards of line have been pulled in and are lying slack between hand and reel. In this case, which frequently arises, the fish must be hooked on a tight line held between finger and rod handle or in the hand, and to start with he must be played with the line held in the hand and being allowed to slip out under light pressure as necessary, while the other hand is used to reel up the slack line as quickly as possible. With practice this too can be done quite easily, though one is apt to breathe a sigh of relief when the slack is all safely accommodated on the reel!

This control of the water-speed of the fly is one of the most important aspects of fishing, and I recommend any fisherman who has not already done so to give it careful consideration.

10
Playing Fish

Much has already been said and written on this subject, but so often on any salmon river one sees hooked fish being badly mishandled by so many different fishermen that possibly some additional words here may not come amiss.

Playing a fish is sometimes branded as being the dullest part of the whole process of capturing him. In certain cases this disparagement may well be true, though doubtless few beginners would agree with it!

I remember a certain well-known fisherman on the Cork Blackwater who, as soon as he had hooked a salmon, used at once to hand the rod over to his ghillie, and apart from handling the gaff took no further part in the proceedings. And one has heard of others who adopted elsewhere this procedure. It is not perhaps too difficult to understand this, though indeed I would not myself subscribe to it.

A lot surely depends on the type of river and the type of fish. For instance to play a small spring salmon of 7 to 9lb. on strong tackle in a deep sluggish river, when the water is cold (and the fish consequently inactive), can hardly be classed as a *great* thrill, particularly for the experienced fisherman. The achievement, he probably feels, is three-quarters completed once the fish is hooked, and it only remains to get it on the bank as soon as possible in order to continue fishing with the hope of shortly catching another and possibly better fish. To go to the other end of the scale, how about playing even a moderate sized Norwegian salmon of say 35lb., let alone one of 10 or 20lb. bigger, in a foaming rock-strewn torrent the size of the Spey but twice as fast? Who could call that dull, when the chances of landing such a fish are about three to one against, however strong the tackle used, and when the fight may take an hour or more of hard physical endurance?

The play in such different instances, it must be admitted, has very little in common; and between two such extremes lie contests of all types, according to the nature of river and fish, from the humdrum to the hair-raising. One thing emerges quite obviously at this stage from thoughts about playing salmon, and that is that unless the fish has a fair chance of escape for one reason or another the thrill is lacking. (Does anyone get much excitement from pulling in mackerel on a handline?) And the bigger the salmon, and the more obstructions there are in the river, the greater is the satisfaction in successfully landing him.

It is fair to say that if one sees a hooked fish splashing madly and turning cartwheels on the top of the water, it is almost certainly being badly handled. Equally if a fish of no great size, in normal circumstances and hooked on tackle of reasonable strength, takes an inordinate time to land, and is described as 'sulking', this too is being badly handled. The happy medium is what should be sought after.

The experienced horsemaster cultivates the use of 'hands' in the control of his mount. There is a similar quality in the control of fish. Beginners are often told 'to keep a steady strain on him'. This advice may be alright for those in the early stages of fishing, and for the young, but I think the counsel of my former Spey ghillie Willie Craik was better. He used to say: 'When *he* pulls, you let him run, but when he stops pulling then *you* pull'. Simple words but meaningful. While the fish is still full of energy and go, it is hard to control him; and indeed if there are snags and obstacles in the offing to try and hold him too hard may do more harm than good. But as and when he shows signs of weakening, then is the time to put on the strain.

Beginners are also told to 'keep the rod up'. This also is good advice, and a fish that pulls hard should be allowed to run line freely off the reel, rather than to pull the rod tip down so that cast line and rod are drawn into a nearly straight line and the advantage of flexibility in the rod is lost. On the other hand I have found that it is often better to keep the rod almost horizontal when playing fish, pointing preferably downstream. Provided the rod in this position is kept fully bent, the advantage of flexibility is not sacrificed. By holding the rod thus a greater degree of side-strain is exerted on the fish, and such a strain is what kills him most quickly. His method of swimming in the water, even if he is stationary in a current, is serpentine, from side to side, horizontally. Side strain, if continued, tends all the time to throw him off balancc, whereas strain from overhead is far more akin to an effort to draw a cork out of a bottle. But it might be dangerous to tell a beginner to hold his rod horizontally, so for such a person I would not suggest this. One drawback to holding the rod in the horizontal position is that it makes it easier for a strong and active fish to get the line 'drowned' (of which more hereafter). So it is perhaps not wise to adopt this position too soon after the fish is first hooked; and if the fish shows signs of starting to make a determined run away from the angler it is also wiser to shift the rod quickly to the vertical position in order to keep as much line as possible clear of the water.

One often hears of fish 'sulking', and in this connection is reminded of the story of Bishop Browne of Bristol who played a large salmon in thc Tay cstuary, many years ago now, for over ten hours before losing him. One wonders in such a case who was playing who! (In contrast Miss Ballantine landed her 64lb. fish at Glendelvine also on the Tay in a mere two hours.) I think that 'sulking' should only occur, or be allowed to occur in quite exceptional circumstances, such as when a large fish is hooked on impossibly light tackle, or where it is impossible to follow a heavy fish downstream, in a strong current. It is often the result of an inexperienced fisherman being 'frightened' of his fish, failing to realise how much strain his tackle will stand, and failing to exert it. Never be 'frightened' of a salmon—hustle him, and bustle him from different angles, and keep him on the move. Side strain as described above will almost always prevent him from sulking. Don't let him lie still and husband his strength; the worst position for the angler to take up is upstream of his fish, holding him steady in the current. The fish thus hangs, almost without effort, and he can do this indefinitely without becoming tired. I once played a fish of around 28lb. at Bindon in the Dorset Frome for two hours in this way, and could do nothing with him. There was a low bridge five yards downstream from where I hooked him (on a large fly and 15lb. B.S. nylon!). He had to be stopped from going under this bridge; but the river, although only seven yards wide at that point was deep and fast, and I could not get him to run upstream. I put as much strain on him as my tackle would stand all that time, and my rod was a 15 foot split cane and powerful. He simply hung in the mid-river and would not move, though he jumped twice so I could estimate his weight. He showed no signs of tiring and eventually the fly came away. If I had been able to pull him downstream I would no doubt have landed him in twenty minutes or less.

If you are not certain how much strain your tackle will stand, it is a good tip to hook your fly or bait into a fence post or a low branch, run out a fair length of line off the reel mounted on your rod as for fishing, then pull with your rod as on a fish, and see how much strain you can exert without your cast breaking. You may be surprised; and this procedure ought to give you confidence when subsequently you hook fish.

In small rivers, playing small fish or even large ones is comparatively easy unless there are unwonted obstructions in the river bed or on its banks. There is seldom room for fish to run out a long line, and so increase the strain on the leader or hook hold; they are unlikely to get snagged however active they are; and there is not usually a powerful streamy current to help them.

It is in rivers of medium size with a strong flow (for example the Aberdeenshire Dee from Invercauld downstream) that play starts to become more intricate; and the larger the fish the knottier the problem. Fish of medium size say 15–20lb. are sometimes more active it is true, but the larger the fish the bigger his reserves of resistance and the longer, as a rule, he will take to land. During that time the risk of the hook hold giving way is always on the increase, and other mishaps can always occur. Increase in the size of river, strength of flow, and size of fish all tend to make playing the fish more and more difficult, until as depicted above one arrives at some such river as the Sundal, Rauma, Evanger, or Aaro in Norway which would seem to offer what is pretty well the ultimate problem in landing salmon. Several times on the Sundal I remember my fly being unexpectedly taken and my rod top being savagely pulled down, on the edge of a long, foaming, and rock strewn torrent, the only immediate reaction in my mind being the thought 'Oh! my God, what now?'

There are many points to be borne in mind over appropriate action in such a case. One of the first and most important is to avoid by all possible means allowing the fish to get the line 'drowned'. Where the river is wide and the central current strong this may not be easy and at times will be impossible; more difficult too with a thick dressed fly-line than with a thin bait line. One can only offer the advice, if there appears to be danger of 'drowning', to keep the rod as high as possible, and keep as much line out of the water as possible. To encourage the fisherman to 'hold on tight' at this stage may be a mistake. It may only induce the fish, if he is still full of energy, to run harder. One can only say keep up a reasonable strain, and ease it off if you feel the salmon responds by slowing up. If, however, he is already half beat, then by all means put on the full strain.

If he is wading deep it may well pay the fisherman not to come ashore to start with, but to stay well out in the river, wading upstream if necessary, and so to keep his line over and clear of the main central rush. Alternatively it may be preferable to come ashore, if there is a high bank behind. The angler can then climb to the top of this as soon as possible after hooking his fish and play him from a high vantage point; this too will probably save him from being 'drowned'. But if in spite of all his efforts he does get 'drowned', and in a big river with strong fish it happens to all of us from time to time, there is still good hope of a successful outcome to the struggle if he is patient and plays his cards well. It is important to watch for the moment when the weight of the line in the current becomes too strong for the fish to tow it behind him any longer. He will then probably splash or jump, and turn abruptly downstream, and the angler will feel the line suddenly go slack. He should then reel in as quickly as he possibly can, walking downstream at the same time, and so make every effort to keep the line as taut as possible. Probably the fish will move downstream too quickly for him, and a certain amount of slack line will develop, which cannot be helped. There is a danger of slack so formed becoming snagged in obstructions, so the quicker the line is taken in the better.

Being 'drowned' is always better avoided. In these circumstances there must be a moment, or a longer period of time, when the angler is no more in direct contact with his fish. This always is liable to lead to disaster in the form of the hook dropping out of the fish's mouth, the leader broken by the fall of a heavy fish jumping, or by the line or leader becoming snagged round an obstruction; one has seen it and had it happen so often; nevertheless as pointed out above being 'drowned' by no means necessarily entails losing the fish, and in perhaps five cases out of six good handling will retrieve the situation.

In general, whether on big, medium, or small rivers, a lot of overall principles apply to playing fish, of which the angler should automatically and unthinkingly bear in mind. For example it is as well not to try to play fish on too short a line. By reeling in too far the angler loses the elasticity of a fair length of line out, and the fish may well panic if drawn too soon into shallow water. For him as a result to kick and splash violently on such a short line is undesirable and may lead to his escape. It is also undesirable that he should indulge in jumps, and the more vigorous these are the greater the likelihood of hook being thrown or leader being broken. A fish is often liable to jump, it may be impossible to stop him doing so. On the other hand the cause of this is frequently that he is being held on too tight a line. The angler can often sense when the fish is 'limbering up' to jump, and if he at once eases the pressure he will find the fish eases up too, and instead of jumping sinks back deeper in the stream. Here is another case of the beneficial exercise of 'hands' in the handling of fish.

If the fish does jump, however, as we have all been told, the proper course is immediately to drop the rod point, so that the fish does not fall back on a tight leader when he re-enters the water, and so does not break it or tear out the hook. This is without doubt advisable and to be commended. It certainly should be done; though it may easily be overlooked, and I know that I for one am culpable in this respect from time to time. When a long line is out, and when the line is drowned, it may make little difference and be impossible in any case to ease the pressure on the leader; but this is no excuse for failing to attempt to do this, and with a medium or short line in play dropping the rod point certainly *does* make a difference and in no circumstances should be omitted.

One other small point worth remembering is this. If a salmon is being played on a shortish line, with the angler knee-deep in the water, the latter should remember to keep his feet close together. It is very embarrassing for him otherwise if the fish makes a sudden dive between his legs, which can lead to every sort of difficulty. Such misfortunates have been known to happen.

If the fish hooked is reckoned to be a big one he should be played hard whenever possible, and there should be no let-up on him in deference to his size. If possible the angler should keep below him, and make him fight both the weight of the current and the pressure of the line combincd. In the case of a really big fish, say of 30lb. or over, I would be prepared to pull him half a mile or more downstream, provided there were no obstructions. He would be more quickly killed in this way. If I was using strong tackle I would also be prepared at intervals and when it became necessary to drop the rod point low and almost handline the fish. Much greater pressure, if so wanted, can be exerted in this way, though it needs careful manipulation.

If the fish is known or estimated to be lightly hooked, and one can sometimes gauge this from the manner in which he takes or from the sight of a hook precariously fixed on the edge of his mouth, it is as well to handle him very carefully, and to keep downstream of him as much as possible in order to draw the hook back into the angle of his jaw. It will be a bad moment if he turns his head downstream and shakes it. Many a fish has been lost at such a moment, but as far as I can see there is little to be done in counteraction, except to ease the pressure and on no account to hold too hard until the fish has once more turned his head in the opposite direction. Then is the time to pull harder in the hope that if the hook does come away it will rehook itself in a firmer position further back in the fish's mouth.

Some mention should here be made about 'walking up' a fish. If there is some reason, such as rapids or obstructions downstream, for inducing a fish to swim upriver, it is usually not too difficult to make him do this by walking up. With a fair length of line out, one can usually get him to follow steadily upstream by keeping a steady pressure on him and walking up the bank, towing him behind one like a dog on a lead. Every time he protests by turning away or kicking one has to pause until he becomes quiet when one can continue the process. One can often progress 100 or 150 yards upstream, if necessary, in this fashion. It is usually said that one should not attempt to turn the reel if one wants to walk a fish up for fear of the vibration of the check upsetting him, but simply put ones fingers firmly on the reel drum and keep going. It may well be easier that way and more effective. On the other hand when a fish has run out a long line downstream with perhaps half the backing out, but has finally turned, it is often possible to reel him up onto a short line again without moving one's feet, if one wants to do this. It doesn't seem that in such a case he pays any attention to the check. Needless to say if one is fishing from a boat, it is even easier to tow a fish upstream with the boatman either rowing or pulling up on a rope. Fish seldom refuse to follow thus.

Occasionally one finds fish are taking really well, and there is good prospect of a sizeable bag in the day. On such auspicious occasions, which in Britain occur only too rarely, it must pay to play one's fish hard in order to land them in the shortest possible time. Five or six minutes saved in the time taken playing each fish might mean a considerably increased bag at the end of the day. Losses, if fish are taking greedily, will probably be negligible. Other occasions when it pays to land fish as quickly as possible are when good taking time is likely to be limited, for instance in early spring during the short period of milder weather towards mid-day, or during the short early morning in summer before a blazing sun minimizes one's chances. A foul hooked fish on a good fishing day is better broken off at once rather than being allowed to take up valuable time in prolonged play.

Grilse are something of a problem. They should be played very lightly on small and extra sharp hooks. Their mouths are soft and they twist, kick and turn to an amazing degree. Their play resembles that of sea trout, except that they endure longer. One needs a light rod and a light hand. Beaching them is the best way of landing them, if a decent beach is handy; or failing that it is best to use a landing net. Whatever precautions are taken however it seems that nearly half of them, when hooked, are likely to escape in one way or another. Nevertheless skilled handling and appropriate tackle will go far in reducing the losses.

Whether one is playing salmon or grilse, there is one final step which is well worth taking. When the fish has become tired and the moment of landing him draws near, it pays then to shift the rod button from one's stomach, where it should have been positioned during the play so far, and to hold the rod in both hands, one above the reel with fingers holding the line against the rod handle, and one below. The fish is likely by then to be on a fairly short line, and a rod held in this way gives better resilience and control in the final stages. If the fish splashes or does anything sudden and unforeseen, the angler is much better placed to control the situation with the rod so held, and if necessary the line can be instantly released.

At all times needless to say there should be an ample length of sound backing on the reel, free to run out without jamming whenever wanted, and line and backing should always be wound in in kite-string fashion, shifted from side to side on the reel drum, to make sure there will be no hitches when it is next run out.

As to checks on the reel, the normal pawl and ratchet check should be adjusted to the right strength, not so stiff that the line cannot run out freely when the fish pulls, nor so light that if the fish runs quickly the reel is liable to over-run and the line to jam. I lost a fish through this in the Tay last season. I knew the check on my reel was too light, but I persisted with it, counting on my fingers to act as an efficient additional brake if I hooked a fish. This I did, in a strong stream. He tore off a strip of line, my fingers slipped, the reel spun, the line jammed, and the fish went free. It all happened in less than five seconds. Such mishaps make one feel small! But with a check at medium tension and with the tips of one's fingers on the line and drum, as an additional brake when required, there is no reason why anything should go wrong. The check by itself should be just powerful enough to stop the reel over-running, and no stronger. Finally the angler should make sure that his reel fittings are efficient and holding the reel securely in position on the rod. There is nothing more aggravating than a loose reel at any time, let alone when a fish is being played. If the reel then comes off there is every likelihood that the fish will do likewise. Such a misfortune caused the loss of one of the biggest fish ever hooked on the Spey. This was in Pol Arder on the Lower Pitchroy beat in September 1954. This fish was estimated at 60lb. (+), and was played for an hour, before loosely adjusted reel fittings allowed the reel to fall off with consequent disaster.

One last word of advice about playing fish. At all times the angler should keep cool and collected, and never allow excitement get the better of his self-control. Time enough when the fish is safely on the bank to give vent to his feelings. Nothing should be done in blind haste, which usually defeats its own object.

After all, except in the case of a specimen fish of 35lb. or so, does it really matter so badly if the fish is lost after a fair fight? Good luck to him! However shattered the angler may feel at the time, there will surely be more fish to come; and will not the triumph of the next successful capture be all the sweeter?

11

Landing Fish

> 'Hey, mon, sic a fish!'
>
> He then went for a stone to fell him with; but . . . the fish began to wamble towards the water, and Kerse turned, and jumped upon it; over they both tumbled, and they, hook, line, and all went into the Tweed. Scrope *Days and Nights of Salmon Fishing* (1843)

Landing fish neatly with a minimum of time lost, and a minimum of fuss and bother is an art worth studying. The above quotation from Scrope can be taken as an awful warning about what can happen in the case of mishandled 40 pounders, such as this one was said to be.

Never attempt to land your hooked fish until he is well played out, and has ceased to kick or thrash. This is certainly a guiding principle which, except in certain special circumstances to be noted hereafter, should govern all your initial outlook on this operation; and being sound advice you will ignore it at your peril. There is nothing more humiliating than to lose a good fish at the last moment, not so much through the hook coming away, which is always a fair sporting possibility, as through some blunder (probably caused by impatience) which involves a cut or broken leader or line.

But as soon as the fish shows signs of being well tired you can turn your thoughts towards landing him without unnecessary delay. Always bear in mind that so long as he is still in the water there is always a chance of his getting away; and you can never be fully sure of him until he is safely on the bank and knocked hard on the head.

The signs of tiredness are fairly obvious; 'his head comes up', as one's ghillie says, he begins more and more to turn on his side and eventually, perhaps, belly upwards for a moment or two, if he completely loses control; and he no longer has the energy to jump out or dive deep or even make a run of any distance. Though he still may be capable of feebly kicking or thrashing on or near the surface, all his movements become weaker and slower.

To get him in close to the bank you may now find it a good move to walk back away from the river, if there is room, towing him shorewards with your reel drum held fast. Then advance towards him, reeling in as you go, to repeat the whole process with a shorter line. But always be ready to release the tension if he makes a sudden determined effort to run out again.

Assuming now that all has gone well and you estimate your fish to be tired enough, you have the choice of three effective different ways of landing him, and of one or two others not so good. *Gaffing* is the best known method and the widest used. The history of the gaff as an auxiliary instrument for landing salmon dates back a long way, and is interesting to trace. For example in *Barkers Delight* (1657) the author advises his readers to have a 'good large landing hook to take him' (the salmon) 'up'. And in Franck's *Northern Memoirs* (1658) we read, with reference to the landing of salmon: 'Another expedient is the landing rod' (gaff) 'which I rather approve of.' These are the earliest known references to the use of the gaff.

As to the gaff itself, which you are to use, provided that shaft, fittings, and hook are strong, that the gape is not less than 2¾ inches, and that the point is sharp, it will do. A further refinement is to have the gaff head chromiumed. This certainly is an asset in preventing rust and keeping the metal clean. If the shaft is long enough to be used as a wading stick, fitted with a leather carrying strap and a weighted toe cap on the butt end, the gaff will serve a dual purpose. In any case the extra reach provided by a long shaft is useful, particularly when one is gaffing one's own fish, and short telescopic gaffs are not so effective. One word of warning—avoid the separate gaff head that screws into the socket at the end of a shaft. Sooner or later the screw fitting is sure to work loose, and this will land you in trouble just at the crucial moment when you are trying to gaff a fish, as the gaff head will turn unexpectedly.

There used to be a certain well beloved ghillie on the Spey, who was very proud of his home-made gaff, the head of which started life as the tine of a garden fork. As its owner used to say, this was 'mighty fine' for gaffing small fish of 13lb. or less, and this gaff head never straightened out by more than about 45 degrees (he used to bend it back into shape as soon as the fish was safely on the bank). But the trouble started when anything much bigger than this was gaffed, and this horrible instrument used to straighten right out with the weight of the fish upon it. There would then be a hectic scene, with the fish falling off on to the bank if one was lucky, but more likely back into the river, when the ensuing drama can be left to the imagination. Needless to say, one wants to do better than this in providing oneself with a reliable gaff head!

1 Fishing the Graveyard, a good pool on the Lochy; water very low, in July. The fisherman is quite rightly wading in no further than necessary, covering the water adequately and not frightening the fish.

A floating line with a small lightly dressed fly of around size 8 is the best outfit. It can be fished in the orthodox way, though the fly skimming across the surface with a small V can also be effective in streamy or ripply water.

2 Dailuaine, a first class pool on the Spey at Wester Elchies; the river at summer level in June. A floating line with a small fly is best, (though a bigger fly at dusk or in a strong stream can be useful).

In this pool fish lie on both sides of the main stream, as well as in the middle of it. A long line is therefore an advantage to cover the outliers.

PLATE 2

3 The Holly Bush, a lovely stretcl
Cambus o'May on the Dee. There is
need to wade in more than a few ya
from the bank.

In a place like the Holly Bush, if
water falls low and the stream sla
ens, it is worth adding to the wa
speed of the fly by stripping line as
fly fishes round, and by shooting i
the next cast.

4 The neck of Waterside, on the Dee at Glen Tanar. This pool is nearly 200 yards long, and will fish from one side or the other at any height. The hill in the far distance is Morven (2862 feet) still snow-covered in April. With the water temperature still cold, fish will prefer the deeper and slacker part of the pool, further downstream.

To consider now the general procedure of gaffing. With the fish suitably tired, the moment for action approaches, and above all the gaffer must keep calm and collected, and not rush it. Nothing is more deplorable than to see a gaff wildly brandished, and ineffective strokes being made by someone who cannot restrain his excitement. Apart from anything else, it is very dangerous. If the taut line or leader passes just for one split second over the sharp point of the gaff head, it will part like cotton.

Choose a good place for gaffing, where a fish can be brought in easily. If you are gaffing for someone else, take up your position there, having taken the cover off the gaff point (this has been forgotten before now!). Get a good foothold and wait. Somewhere where there is a reasonable depth of water is best, as fish hate being drawn into shallow water with their backs out, and fight harder to avoid it. Also choose a place if possible where there is little or no current, as this makes it so much easier to bring the fish in. It is far better, having chosen such a place, that you should encourage the fisherman to bring the fish to you there, rather than for you to go chasing after the fish wherever it may happen to come in. So don't do the latter unless it becomes absolutely necessary. Having taken up your position try to make yourself as inconspicuous as possible by keeping still, and perhaps by bending down. And as the fish starts to come in, hold your gaff out ready over the water, so that you don't have to make a sudden thrust out with it at the last moment. Any such sudden movement with either gaff shaft or arms is liable to frighten the fish at the crucial moment and to make him turn away from you just when you want to have him broadside on. But if the fisherman knows his job and can bring the fish in with a run near the surface, steadily and unresistingly within your range, it is a simple matter to put the gaff quickly and quietly point downwards across the middle of his back, and simply lift. If the point of the gaff is sharp, it will go into him like butter.

One or two points should be further investigated here. Where, for instance, is the best place in the fish's body to put the gaff point home? The answer undoubtedly is as near the centre of his back as possible, taking a good hold, so that the gaff will not tear out, and the fish will hang balanced on it as he is lifted from the water. Too near the tail is bad. The gaff head is likely to get only a shallow hold, and it is possible for an active fish, particularly a small one, to kick himself off the gaff if he is sufficiently energetic. Near the head is better, and the gaff is likely to get a good hold, but this may bring the gaff point in dangerous proximity to the leader if the stroke is missed.

Never try to gaff the fish underneath with the point of the gaff upwards. It is hard to see why anyone recommends this method. Unless the fish is belly upwards, it will only result in his being gaffed in the soft stomach where the gaff is far more likely to tear out, and an upward stroke if the fish avoids it is much more likely to cut the leader. If the gaff does go home, on the other hand, it will probably produce an ugly gaping wound in the fish's belly, whereas if the fish is properly gaffed over the centre of the back the wound will be small and inconspicuous.

So there can be no argument as to the best policy in this respect, and in all normal circumstances you should try for a gaff hold over the back and as central as possible. Only in desperate emergency should you be prepared to put the gaff home anywhere, regardless of where this may be.

Something has already been said about the sort of position that should be taken up by whoever is operating the gaff, preferably where there is reasonably deep water and absence of strong current. And it may be added here that it is an advantage to stand firmly on the bank, if this is possible and consistent with these requirements. But if the water close to the bank is too shallow, the operator may have to wade in a certain distance, though it is unwise to go in too far, as to wade back with a salmon kicking on the end of a gaff is rather a risky business (a preliminary knock on the head with a 'priest' is a wise precaution). Try rather to find a place where the hooked fish can be brought as close to the bank as possible. Having selected such a position, wait till the fish is brought broadside on to you and near the surface. A rod who knows his business, taking his time, will seldom have difficulty in bringing a fish to you in such a way. If you try to short-circuit the business by gaffing the fish when he is still deep in the water and capable of twisting and turning, you do so at your own risk. A skilled and experienced gaffer may bring this off successfully, but not without risk; and it is really better for him to await a more favourable opportunity.

The actual motion of gaffing should definitely be in two stages—first the stroke or 'lift' that, once the gaff has been extended over the fish, puts the gaff point into him as described above, and second the raising of the fish from the water, held securely as one hopes on the gaff head, with the gaff shaft now held perpendicularly. There is no need to rush the second stage; when the gaff head is well home, the fish can be lifted deliberately and unhurriedly, and carried on the gaff to the shore and well up the bank to be given the coup de grâce. Never try to combine these two stages into one sweeping movement, reminiscent of that of a hay rake, in which the fish is gaffed and scooped out onto the bank all in one dramatic coup. Such over-exertion is unnecessary, and only leads to trouble of one sort or another, even if this is no worse than an ugly gash in the fish's side.

One other transgression, strictly to be avoided, is that of gaffing over and across the line or leader. Never do this, as if you attempt to, and you miss the fish or he turns away at the crucial moment, you will either cut the line clear through on the gaff point, or else get it entangled in the gaff head which will land you in great trouble at best. It is true that very dexterous gaff handlers may sometimes bring off this feat successfully, and with the fish safely on the bank there may be some raucous laughter at the risk overcome. All the same to gaff across the line, if persisted in, means certain disaster sooner rather than later. Therefore on principle never do it, but just be a little more patient until the fish comes in the right way round; and if you are gaffing for someone else, in order to reassure him explain to him briefly why you have withheld your stroke. It is worth noting that polaroid glasses are a good help to anyone attempting to gaff a fish, particularly in bright sunshine reflected off the water. In some lights it is very hard to see fish clearly with the naked eye, and polaroids usually make it easier. Their use should not be neglected.

If the fish is not completely played out, he may give a forceful thrash or thrust forward as the gaff is put into him. Be prepared for this, don't be caught napping, and don't on any account drop the gaff. Be sure beforehand that the gaff shaft is not slippery and that you have a good handhold on it. It doesn't much matter which way in your hand you grip the gaff; either point downwards like the stage villain's dagger or upwards like a tennis racquet; but if the latter it means that obviously you will have to turn your wrist round to get the gaff pointing at the right angle when you gaff the fish. So long as you keep your hold firm, you can adopt whichever grip comes easiest to you.

As I have said, the second stage in the motion of gaffing is that of lifting the fish from the water and carrying him on the gaff well inland. This action should, however, be modified in the case of very big fish of say 30lb. or over, when if the slope is not too steep it is safer to 'drag' rather than 'lift'; there is less strain thus both on the gaff and the gaff hold, as the fish is not actually raised off the ground. So when the day comes for you to gaff your next 40 pounder, you may well find it worthwhile to bear this point in mind!

One more word of warning, when you have successfully gaffed your fish it is always a wise move to give him two or three sharp knocks on the head with a 'priest' or killer before you take the gaff head out of him rather than after (also before you remove the hook from his mouth). Many a fish has disconcertingly escaped after being gaffed, because his captor has neglected this elementary precaution; and particularly if the bank slopes steeply it is surprising how quickly an active fish can thrash his way back into the river, if he is not first knocked out before the gaff is removed.

It is worthwhile also considering what your immediate action should be if the worst has happened, and you have 'gaffed' the line rather than the fish—that is with the fish still on the hook you have inadvertently got the line or leader inside the gaff head, and still under tension from the rod point. This ugly situation happens to almost all of us sooner or later. At all costs the line must not be drawn under tension across the sharp gaff point, so that the best thing now is for the rod point to be dropped and the line allowed to go slack until the gaff has been disengaged. This is easy enough for the fisherman to do, when he has a ghillie and is not trying to gaff his own fish, and the ghillie if he keeps calm can get the gaff-hook free from the slackened line without cutting it. But it is another matter when the fisherman is trying to gaff his own fish, and if the fish in addition complicates matters by pulling hard at the same time at the other end. How to free the line then without it being drawn over the gaff point becomes an almost insoluble puzzle, and quick action being necessary it is possibly best to let go of the gaff and hope to retrieve it later. Otherwise you can only trust to the fish being amenable, and somehow allowing you to get your line free. You will need a good deal of luck to extricate yourself successfully from such an awkward situation, so do your best to avoid it in the first place.

So far in this chapter perhaps not enough differentiation has been made between the process of gaffing a fish for someone else, and gaffing your own fish when you are fishing alone. But up to now all that has been said is equally applicable to both. Gaffing for someone else can be more of an anxiety, but at all costs keep calm and don't be hustled, for instance, by an excited tyro *shouting* such heresies as: 'Look, look, now's your chance!' or, 'Quick, quick, for God's sake gaff him now!' Just remain quiet, and await the first good chance that occurs.

On the other hand gaffing your own fish involves perhaps more patience as, particularly with bigger fish, it takes longer to get them on the necessary short line; and incidentally the longer your rod the more difficult this becomes. But however great you exasperation, you must not give way to this on any account. Again, keep calm, take no unnecessary risks, and remember that if the fish is well hooked he won't get off whatever happens, while if he is lightly hooked you will be lucky to get him anyway, and don't grudge him his freedom if he does beat you in the end.

Don't reel up too short, otherwise you will find yourself in the proverbial position of the donkey with the carrot, i.e., you won't be able to bring the fish in close enough to reach him, and as you move towards him the angle of the pull from your rod tip will still keep him out of your reach. You must have a certain minimum length of line out in order to bring him within gaffing range, holding your rod back over your shoulder if necessary.

Also at the actual moment of gaffing, and simultaneously with the gaff point entering the fish, you should remember to slack off line. Some people hold a foot or two of slack line against the rod handle to be released at once, which is quite a good way of doing this. The object is, of course, to take all pressure off the rod tip, which can be snapped if the fish gives a violent kick on a taut line.

One last word of advice; when you are bringing a fish in to the gaff, either to yourself or to someone else, there is no need to lift his head right out of the water as one sometimes sees done. This only puts an unnecessary strain on the hook hold, and may tear the hook out. It is said in support of such procedure that a fish cannot see when his eyes are out of water, and this may well be true. It may therefore be worth while just putting enough upward pull on the line to keep his uppermost eye out of water as he comes in on his side, and fish certainly seem to come in more blindly this way. It needs little extra pressure to achieve this.

Netting with a landing net is an alternative method of landing salmon, and a good one if properly carried out. Like the gaff, the landing net was in use as an auxiliary instrument much longer ago than one might realise, in fact, at least three centuries ago, because Franck mentioned its use in his *Northern Memoirs* (1658) and 'approved' it.

Although the gaff is such an efficient instrument, its main disadvantage is, of course, the wound which it inevitably makes in the fish, and which to some extent spoils it. Also some people are reluctant to give such cavalier treatment as gaffing to a magnificent fish which has given them wonderful sport. In addition the use of gaffs on a number of rivers is definitely forbidden at certain seasons (e.g. on the Tweed in spring and autumn), either as a protection for kelts or else because a gaff is classed as a prohibited poaching instrument. Also if one is blessed with the help of a ghillie who is expert at the job, and who is provided with the right type of landing net (of which more hereafter) netting is, in fact, just as efficient a method as gaffing, which is another mark in its favour. Further, if one is by oneself (or with a ghillie for that matter) and gaffing is prohibited, and if there is no beach where one can adopt the third efficient method of landing salmon (to be mentioned later), one is almost inevitably bound to fall back on netting if one wants to make a workmanlike job of landing one's fish. Nor when one uses a net is there the risk of one's line being cut, as with a gaff, and where grilse or small salmon are concerned it is definitely easier to net them than to gaff them. Such fish are not only spoilt by a gaff mark but they are apt to be active in the water and present a very small and light target for a gaff, i.e., they will not be impaled as easily on a gaff point as a big fish will owing to its weight; and they are more easily missed. There are times and circumstances, therefore, when netting, as opposed to gaffing, definitely comes into its own.

In netting, as with gaffing, a good deal depends on whether the fisherman has a ghillie to help him or whether he is netting his own fish. A ghillie can be equipped with a large and probably home-made landing net, the frame of which will be a strong iron hoop of 2½–3 feet diameter, mounted on a stout wooden shaft of 5 feet or more in length. The actual bag of the net, suspended from this hoop, will be of thick twine or braided nylon with a depth of at least 3 feet, and with a mesh small enough to hold a grilse. Such a net will also hold a 60 pounder if necessary, but while it is easily enough wielded by someone using both hands, it is far too cumbersome for single-handed use. If, therefore, the fisherman has to net his own fish he needs one of the light retractable single-handed metal-framed nets now obtainable at any good fishing tackle dealer, of which the 'Gye' net is an outstanding example. Such nets are easily carried on the back by means of a special leather carrying strap, and are out of the way while one is fishing. And they are good for landing salmon up to around 25lb. If your fish is bigger than this, you will have to await the help of someone with a bigger net or a gaff, or else try to beach him, as described later.

Whichever type of net is used, however, there is one feature which is desirable in all of them, and that is the solid metal hoop frame. This metal hoop is often of great value in acting as a 'scoop' to ensure that fish are gathered into the net and do not fall outside it. Nets which are collapsible, Y shaped, and with a leather strap or chain from arm to arm, are much less effective in this respect.

Braided nylon is the best material for the actual net bag. Ordinary twine rots fairly quickly but nylon lasts for years. Always take care that your net is sound, of ample depth, and has no holes—barbed wire and tree branches seem to have an irresistible attraction for nets; and any damage should be repaired on the spot.

Turning now to the actual process of netting, the first consideration as with gaffing is to choose the best available place for it—it being always better for the fish to be brought under control to such a place, rather than its being left to chance where he arrives when he is finally played out. The first thing needed is reasonably deep water, say 18 inches deep or deeper for choice—it is no use trying to net a fish in a shallow gravelly stickle, as one wants to get the net, which at best is a rather clumsy object, well underneath the fish in order to lift it and bag him. And above all a place with little or no stream should be chosen, as the handling of a net in any sort of current becomes increasingly awkward with additional flow.

If possible the netter should wade into the river for a short distance; it is usually easier to operate like that than off the bank, especially if the bank is a high one. As the fish becomes increasingly tired, and is held near the surface, he should hold the net out with its head well under water, and wait for the fish to be drawn over it or else slide the net quietly but quickly underneath the fish as soon as the latter is within reach. Usually in fact a combination of these two actions is best, and all that is then left to be done is for the net to be raised so that the hoop is above water level and the fish enmeshed in the bag of the net. Usually this process, if the fish is well played out, is quite simple, especially to anyone who is used to netting trout—but at this stage a note of warning should be sounded over three possible mischances that can more easily occur where salmon are concerned. The first is that if a fish is netted tail first it is easy for him to swim out of the net and escape temporarily, until he can be brought in again. So always aim to get his head in the net first rather than his tail, that is to see that it is the front part of the fish that is over the net when you lift it rather than the tail part. With his head in first he will be securely bagged. Secondly, it is important to watch the fish carefully when he is swimming anywhere close to the net, and if there is any likelihood of his hitting the outside of the net, i.e. the 'wrong' side, whip it quickly away. If you fail to do this, and if a hook happens to be exposed outside his mouth, it is odds on that it will catch in the net meshes, and the fish will instantly break free. Lastly, whoever is wielding the net (and this applies also to gaffing) should when standing in the water be careful to keep his legs close together, as already mentioned.

To continue, with the fish safely bagged in the net there is little left to do except to get safely ashore. If a strong double handed net of the 'Tweed' type is being used it matters little how the net is held, either vertically or horizontally. But a thin-framed metal net such as the 'Gye' must be held vertically, otherwise the weight of the fish will bend or buckle the shaft. As soon as the fish is in the net therefore, hold the shaft of such a net perpendicularly and close the net aperture by so doing. There is no need then even to lift the fish out of the water until you get close to the bank.

One thing alone remains—once you are safely ashore with the fish, lay him down and hit him on the head through the meshes, making sure he is dead before you take him out of the net and remove the hook. This is a wise precaution and, as at the same stage in gaffing, it should never be neglected. Then give your net a rinse in the river to remove fish slime, and it is ready for further action.

So much for the overall process of netting and as will be readily appreciated the same general considerations hold good whether you are netting for someone else or single-handed for yourself alone. The only main difference is that in the latter case, as with gaffing, it is more difficult to get your fish onto the necessary length of short line. And the longer your rod and the bigger your fish the more difficult does this process become. But if you select a good position as described, keep calm and patient, and remember to draw the fish towards you rather than go chasing after him, with any luck all will go well for you; though you must, of course, expect it to take longer when you are on your own.

Beaching is another first class method of landing salmon, an alternative to gaffing or netting, which is not known or practised nearly as widely as it might be. Like netting, its main advantage is that it does not inflict a wound on the fish; also it can be carried out without the hooked fish ever getting a glimpse of the fisherman, which may sometimes shorten the length of the struggle.

It goes without saying that the presence of an adequate beach is an essential prerequisite, and this is not always to be found. Be it noted in passing, however, that the term 'beach' does not imply gravel alone, in fact sand or silt is nearly as good, or a grassy bank or rock outcrop. Provided all these have a reasonably smooth surface and have a flat enough gradient in their run down to the water's edge, any of them will do for a 'beach' on which to land your fish. It is surprising at such a spot what little extra tension if any, is needed to make him slip out of the water and along your 'beach' and away from the river. The line need only be taut enough to keep his head pointing inland, and every kick or wriggle he gives will carry him further in that direction, helped by the natural slipperiness of his exterior. This is when the gradient of the 'beach' is nearly flat, but naturally the process becomes more difficult progressively as the gradient becomes steeper, until a point is reached when with the slope too steep beaching becomes impossible. If you want to land your fish by beaching, it is therefore worth having a look round before you start fishing to find one or two such suitable places, and it may be worthwhile taking a hooked fish for a considerable distance up or down stream in order to avail yourself of one of them.

As to the process of beaching, as always you should first get the fish well tired. Then without reeling up too short, keeping him on a length of 10 to 15 yards of line, manoeuvre him opposite the place you have chosen for beaching and gradually work him in towards it, by walking backwards away from the river if there is room to do this. (If there is no room you will have no choice but to reel him in short, though it is better to keep him on a fair length of line if possible. This gives more elasticity if he thrashes or jumps, and also enables you to keep out of his sight.)

Keep his head pointed shorewards if you can, and keep him on the go in that direction without exerting too much pressure which might (and sometimes does!) cause a worn hook hold to give. On no account become too excited at the sight of your prey almost within your grasp, and pull over-hard. In fact, the pressure for choice should be little more than that exerted in the normal course of play. You will find that on the first two or three occasions, when you get him into shallow water, the fish will almost certainly have enough strength left to get his head round in spite of the pull of your line, and thrash his way back into deeper water. But each time he does this it will exhaust him still more, and you will find in due course that you can keep him going in the right direction, with perhaps a little extra pressure, right up onto the beach. Provided you keep his head pointing inland, each kick that he gives will take him further from the water. Keep him going if you can, until you reckon he is far enough on shore to be safe, and until he turns on his side. As long as he is still back up and belly down he can thrash his way along fairly quickly whether in or out of the water; but turning on his side is the signal of surrender. You can then walk up to him, reeling up as you go to keep the line taut and prevent him turning again towards the water, and either knock him on the head with your 'priest' where he lies, or else catch hold of him just above his tail and push him further up the bank (rather than picking him up), before despatching him. In emergency, if the hook comes out at the last moment or if you have to act extra quickly for some other reason, you can even use a foot and kick him up the beach. This is a quicker way of making him secure, and is better than losing him, even if it does not look very artistic.

If the bank is so steep that you cannot push the fish up it and you have no alternative but to pick him up and carry him, look out for the convulsive kick he will give when he first feels the grip of your hand round his tail. Don't allow yourself to be startled by this into dropping him. Really it is better in such a case to give him two or three knocks on the head with your priest beforehand if you can. It is better to do this before picking him up by the tail, as he is less likely to slip out of your grip, particularly if he is a big fish.

Be prepared for last minute mishaps, they do sometimes occur. If a fish gets off in water that is still deep enough for him to swim you have no hope of getting him; but if his back is well out and he is half stranded, you still have a chance to grab him or kick him ashore if you are quick enough. And complications will obviously arise if you are lucky enough to hook a big fish of around 25lb. or more. In theory there should be no limit to the size of fish that can be beached, and strong tackle is a help in the case of big ones. But the bigger the fish the longer drawn out the process is bound to be; and with light tackle the odds must lie heavily in the big fish's favour. A landing net or a gaff wielded by a ghillie is in fact by far the best answer for big ones, or a gaff if the fisherman is on his own.

But taking it all in all beaching is a very sound method of landing all normal sized fish; and in nineteen cases out of twenty, provided the fisherman knows his job and has the advantage of a reasonable beaching place, the process should go off smoothly and without any crisis.

At this stage the question of tailing salmon arises. It may be that the beaching place is not extensive enough for the fish to be drawn further than the mere edge of the river. In this case a firm grip will have to be taken round the 'wrist' of his tail, and he will have to be lifted, or better still slid, away from the river. If the angler can give him a good clout on the head with a priest before attempting this so much the better; but it may not be easy.

It is difficult, using one hand only, to get a firm enough grip round the tail of a big fish of 20lb. or more to lift him. In this case, and with smaller fish too, it is far better to slide him up the bank, if the slope is not too steep, pushing him ahead and away from the river. A fish of almost any size, however big, can be satisfactorily dealt with in this way. The rod can be dropped and both hands used in emergency.

5 Bench Pool at Holne Chase on the Dart. In very clear water like the Dart, the fisherman must do his utmost to keep out of sight of the fish, and a rod of not less than twelve feet is recommended. With the water low and also warm, say at 52°F or warmer, it would be best to use a floating line with a 10lb breaking strain leader and a size 8 or so small fly.

6 Fishing the neck of Tassach, an excellent low-water pool on the Dee. Where the stream is strong there is no need for a long line; with a cast of 45° downstream the current will fish the fly round without any action by the angler, except for him to pull in two or three yards of line at the end of the cast. It may be necessary to make an upstream mend as soon as the line hits the water.

7 The cauld at Rutherford on the Tweed. This cauld, of little more than 4 feet in height, extends from bank to bank with a partial break at its far end. Caulds such as this, originally built to provide water power for mills, are of considerable value where fishing is concerned, providing good holding water above and below them.

At Rutherford a long slack piece of water above the cauld fishes well from a boat. Below, two good streamy pools fish well in medium or low water.

8 Fishing from an anchored boat on the Spey. This picture shows the normal method of boat fishing on this river.

The boatman's task is to control the boat and let it down the pool on the right line, neither too far out nor too near in, letting go a yard or two of rope (in normal circumstances) between each cast. If a fish is hooked the boat will be brought into the bank, so that the rod can step ashore and play her fish from there.

A good grip depends on having a strong hand and holding the fish absolutely firmly without relaxing. Some anglers advocate a grip facing tailwards, i.e. with the thumb and forefinger nearest the fish's tail. I must admit I have never tried this, because I have always found the opposite hold perfectly satisfactory, i.e. with the thumb and forefinger towards the fish's head. I have tailed a good many hundreds if not thousands of fish in this way, and cannot remember ever having dropped one (though I must have done so!). So I see no reason to alter this method, or to advise anyone else to adopt a different grip.

In addition one has occasionally heard the advice that a handkerchief should be wrapped round the hand before the fish is grasped, in order to prevent slipping, or that a glove should be used. I can only say that I have never found such expedients necessary, though if there is sand nearby it may be an advantage to smear some on the hand.

Lastly we come to the situations where the bank is steep, and the water close to the side is deep, and where there is no beaching place within reasonable distance. Obviously here a net or gaff is badly wanted; but what to do if by some oversight neither of these is available? In this case the fish will have to be lifted out by hand, which is no easy task, especially if it is a big one. The first necessity is to play him right out until he is dead to the world. Then get him right to the bank with his head at the surface—(note that if you can keep his head in the air for a length of time he will 'drown' for lack of oxygen, but this may take an inconveniently long time). Kneel down on the bank and slide your hand quietly down his body, until you can get a firm grip round the 'wrist' of his tail. Then slide him up the bank as best you can. This process is a risky one so I advise you not to forget your gaff or landing net.

An alternative method, which I am assured is possible, is to put a finger or two fingers inside his gill cover, and draw him out head first. I have personally never tried this, or rather have never had to, but I don't fancy it! I can see a variety of unfortunate possibilities occurring, as doubtless the reader also can, if he gives the matter any thought.

So much for the three main methods of landing salmon. That supreme success can be obtained with all of them there is absolutely no doubt. For example the 64 pounder caught by Miss Ballantine at Glendelvine on the Tay in 1922 was gaffed, in common with most British outsized specimens. Mr Pryor's record Tweed fish of 57½lb. caught at Floors in 1886 was, however, netted, it being October when gaffs are there prohibited. There are also at least five other Tweed 50 pounders on record, all of which are likely to have been netted. As for beaching, Jock Scott in *Game Fish Records* (1936) relates how Johann Aarven on the Aaro in Norway in 1921 killed a 69½ pounder, 'which he tailed himself'. This was presumably after having first beached it, as it would seem impossible to lift by hand such a vast fish directly from water of any depth. What a feat this last must have been, and how one longs to have witnessed it.

But there are other methods of landing salmon which are worthy of mention. For instance some fishermen like using a wire 'tailer', a well-known instrument involving a cable noose or snare, which has to be 'cocked' and then slid along the fish's body to grip it either midway or near the tail when it is sharply pulled. It is true that tailers can be made to work reasonably effectively by some people, and they have the advantage of being light and easy to carry when uncocked. Nevertheless their drawbacks are many; for instance, the fish has to be played out to dead still before it is in any way easy to get the tailer round it, and any sort of stream makes tailers awkward to handle. Also if they do slip off the fish, and this easily happens if they are not properly used, the whole process of recocking the tailer, manoeuvring the fish into position, and getting the tailer round it has to be gone through again. In addition it is possible for the noose of the tailer, if badly handled, to slip over the head of the fish, in which case the position at once becomes ludicrous as it is the leader which is now 'tailed', and the only hope of landing the fish is to abandon the tailer altogether. A further drawback is that the thin wire of the noose will sometimes cut into the body of the fish and cause a wound.

So altogether tailers are better avoided, and gaffing, netting, or beaching are far preferable.

There is often a temptation to try to short-circuit the whole process, and by dexterous handling of rod, gaff or net to get the fish safely ashore in quick time before he is properly played out. But this is really not a wise course, and the only time it may pay dividends is on one of those rare red letter days when fish come and get hooked almost as quickly as one can get the line into the water. Also in the case of a monster, say in the 40lb. or over class, every chance with the gaff, however remote, should be taken as it is always odds on such a fish escaping if the play follows its normal course lasting perhaps for hours. In this connection one is reminded of Mrs Morrison's 61lb. fish from the Deveron in 1924. This fish was hooked on a fly on the Mountblairey beat, and swam close in under the bank within six minutes of being hooked.

The ghillie by a skilful piece of gaffing had it out on the bank. And if anyone wants to read a really heart-rending and epic story of a monster lost through the gaffer's lack of initiative, let him turn to the chapter on 'Salmon Fishing' in W. Bromley Davenport's book *Sport* (1885), perhaps the most exciting drama about fishing ever written.

One other occasion when one should do one's best, at least with the gaff, to get the fish on shore as quickly as possible is when the fish is believed to be very lightly hooked. Perhaps the hook in course of play has been seen protruding from his mouth and only holding by a thin morsel of gristle, or perhaps the hook is very small and fine one that cannot be expected to take a strong hold, or perhaps the fish has taken very gingerly after plucking two or three times. Such evidence of a weak hold makes one anxious to lose no chance with gaff or net, even though one dares not put extra pressure on the line.

So there are times, it is true, that when landing fish one needs to act quickly and even prematurely, but as a general rule let your motto be 'Festina Lente'; take your time, keep calm, and don't take unnecessary risks. More fish are certainly lost by undue haste in attempting to land them than vice versa, and after all is it such a disaster if after a good fight a fish does get away with it? At least one hopes that for the fisherman, as for the recipient of the advice 'Never run after a woman or a bus', there will be another one along shortly!

One last thought—having safely landed your fish, never fail to retie the knot to your fly or bait. This should be a hard and fast rule.

12

Salmon That Are Lost

Isaac Walton said that no man can lose what he never had. No doubt the Great Master was perfectly right in what he said, but was it not a mere brown trout which he seems, somewhat carelessly, to have allowed to break him? and that in the midst of three brace of others safely brought to the bank (on worm). One wonders what his reaction would have been to the similar loss of a 30lb. salmon! But then it seems he never was a salmon fisher.

Indeed there is every need to be philosophical about the loss of fish, the possibility of which is the only thing that makes playing them any fun. It is essential for a proper enjoyment of the sport that, strive against it as one will, some should escape from time to time. It makes the capture of those that follow all the sweeter. Nevertheless where one might cross swords with Isaac about this is when one loses a fish through some unpardonable piece of carelessness, and this in fact is what in four cases out of five a break amounts to. It may be caused by a wind-knot, a knot carelessly tied, wear on the leader, backing becoming rotten or jammed on the reel, the reel check being too weak so that the reel over-runs, unsound hooks being used or tackle far too light—these catastrophes are all the direct fault of the angler, and there are many more possible ones like them. He should endeavour to avoid them at all costs; no trouble is too great, and he should kick himself hard if and when they occur. On the other hand when a fish comes unhooked and goes free through no fault of the angler, or when he gains his liberty through entanglement with a snag, in spite of every conceivable effort to keep him clear of it, in fact if the loss is unavoidable and in no way blameworthy, the fisherman has nothing with which to reproach himself. It is all part of the great game in which he is lucky enough to be taking part.

It has been said that no one catches a lot of fish unless he loses a lot too. This may partly be true, as it simply implies that a lot of fish are hooked; and it is the sort of remark that comes handily to a ghillie's list of quotes when he attempts to console an inexperienced rod over a disconcerting loss. But surely part of the thoughtful angler's order of business is to try persistently to reduce all such losses to the bare minimum? Thus does he exercise what must be a large part of his art.

Now the proportion of such losses normally *can* be reduced. It is simply a question of taking pains, coupled with experience, i.e. a process of trial and error. And would not most salmon fishers agree that there is as much to be learnt from fish lost as there is from fish landed, and that the lost ones are apt to remain more firmly implanted in one's memory, especially if they are reckoned outsized?

It may be that, once a fair number of fish have been caught by him, the angler no longer obtains the original thrill in playing a fish which he experienced as a novice. Elsewhere in this book I have already related the story of my friend on the Blackwater who, as soon as he hooked a fish, invariably handed the rod straightaway to his ghillie. He is not the only one by all accounts who has adopted this strange procedure. Nevertheless most fishers prefer to hang on to their rod through thick and thin until the final moment of triumph or disaster; and, what is more, every one of us has his 'big fish story', in which through a curious quirk of similarity the monster is almost invariably lost! It adds so greatly to the effect of the story if the listeners are left hanging on a cliff edge of uncertainty as to a weight which can never satisfactorily be verified.

Many fish are lost, as already pointed out, through the carelessness of the angler; and the elementary faults as listed above can be simply remedied, so there is no point in dwelling on them further. Inexperience, too, in addition to carelessness, lies at the root of many losses. It is often as easy for a novice to hook a 40 pounder as it is for an accomplished performer; and the sudden realization that one has a 'portmanteau' at the end of one's line is an unnerving one for anybody. The novice is likely to fall into one of two alternative traps, either to hold the fish far too lightly, being as it were frightened of it, with the fish taking charge rather than vice versa (one is reminded of the Bishop Browne story on the estuary of the Tay which is related in my *Great Salmon Rivers of Scotland*), or else to clamp down unmercifully which, unless the strongest tackle is being used, is again to court disaster.

For playing very big fish strong tackle with sizeable hooks is essential, let there be no doubt of that; and there should be plenty of elbow room, so that the angler is free to pull his fish well downstream and kill him all the quicker by doing so. To hook a big fish in a small pool in a big and fast river, with strong rapids downstream, followed perhaps by an impassable fall in due course, is a traumatic experience, frequently ending in disaster. The Spey, as British rivers go, is a bad one for playing big fish. Certainly in its lower reaches there are big and long pools, such as the Rock Pool on the Brae Water, Cairnty at Orton, Beaufort, Two Stones, and Holly Bush at Delfur, the Boat Pool at Wester Elchies, and Blacksboat Pool at Upper Pitchroy, amongst others, where there is room to handle a big fish; but so many of its other pools are comparatively small and fast running throughout. No fish of 30lb. or over can be held in them (except by a miracle), let alone a monster in the 40lb. class. One is due, if one hooks such a beast in such a place, for a very rough scramble for many hundred yards down a craggy bank, with the fish tearing ahead at the end of a hundred or more yards of line and backing, through rapids strewn with scattered rocks, and the white water spouting between them. It is heavily odds on the fish in such circumstances, as any experienced Spey fisher will confirm, and made worse by the fact that from May onwards in the Spey one normally uses fairly light tackle, nylon of 12lb. breaking strain or less, and hooks of size 5 or less. This is what is wanted for the average sized Spey fish, but it is too light for 30 or 40 pounders.

Rivers such as the Tweed, Wye, or Hampshire Avon, lend themselves much more readily to the landing of big fish. Their currents are far less strong, nor are there nearly so many obstructions either on the bank or in the river. A fish can usually be followed for an indefinite distance, if this becomes necessary.

Norwegian rivers present a much more menacing problem. Their current is usually stronger than anything in Britain, and their fall fiercer. They are also plentifully endowed with rocks, both sunken and otherwise. Big fish in them thus become formidable antagonists. Nevertheless to some extent this is counter-balanced by the fact that one goes into the struggle with one's eyes open, in that one *expects* big fish, and therefore is well equipped to deal with them. One uses nylon, for instance, of 30 pound or more breaking strain, together with strong and large hooks. Even so one is broken from time to time.

I have said that everyone has his or her story of monster fish lost. One of the most dramatic was that of my great friend, the late Colonel J. P. Moreton, who was fishing the Lower Pitchroy beat on the Spey in September 1954. It was late in the season and fish were getting red. Nevertheless on this occasion they were taking quite well, as sometimes they do when the water temperature drops, and Pat Moreton was using a No.6 double hooked fly on 8lb. breaking strain monofilament, with a light rod. One day in the neck of Pol Arder he and his friends saw a monstrous fish jump, so enormous that they christened it 'the yacht', and they saw it more than once, never thinking they would have further dealings with it as the pool was full of fish at the time. But the next day the inevitable happened, and this leviathan annexed Pat Moreton's fly. Of the subsequent contest there is not a lot to be said. It lasted an hour. Pat Moreton had caught six forty-pounders during his fishing career, so he knew well what a big fish was like; but he said this fish was a good deal bigger than any of them. At one moment it swam right round in the water at only a few yards distance from him and his lady companion; they could see it clearly and its size took their breath away. It was impossible to put any worthwhile pressure on such a monster with the light tackle used, and it appeared hardly to notice that it had been hooked. Eventually owing to sad mischance the line jammed on the reel, and the nylon was broken like cotton. The fish was never seen again—what a tragedy!

Norway is the home of outsized salmon. If anyone wants to read a completely thrilling account of a fight with and the loss of a huge Norwegian fish, the forty-three pounder killed that same morning being described by the ghillie as only 'a small piece of this one', I advise him to read the salmon fishing chapter in *Sport* by W. Bromley-Davenport. This story to my mind is unsurpassable as a drama of salmon fishing.

No doubt the number of huge fish lost in Norway is legion—in spite of the heavy tackle used the odds in most cases are still on the fish. I lost two on the Bjora myself, both of which were put at over 50lb. This was through no fault of my own. I had strong tackle and held on as hard as I could; but both snagged me in previously unlocated sunken tree roots and broke free. The Sundal was another river where losses at times were inevitable. The current was tempestuously strong, and there were bunkers in the shape of impassable rapids or derelict timber salmon traps that caused inevitable breaks if fish entered them. They sometimes had to be held to breaking point on nylon of over 30lb. breaking strain in the attempt to stop them doing this, and this was by no means always successful. One might as well have tried to hold a mustang on a leading rein!

13

The Dry-Fly

Why if salmon will take a dry-fly readily in Canada will they not do so here? In discussing this question I am conscious of treading on rather quaky ground, as I have myself never caught a salmon on a proper dry-fly as one normally understands the term.

I have however seen five fish caught on dry-fly, fished upstream in the generally accepted fashion—but this was in Iceland, and these fish were caught only after prolonged efforts with many repeated casts over them. As to the dry-fly in Britain, there is only one river where I have heard of it being used with any success, and that is the Test. Major G. L. Ashley-Dodd's book *A Fisherman's Log* (1929) has an opening chapter on Dry-Fly Fishing for Salmon. In this he describes salmon being caught on a mayfly in the Test above Romsey, and does not appear to reckon the process unduly difficult. Early dry-fly experiments on salmon apparently were carried out as far back as 1907 and thereafter—usually when the mayfly were hatching and the salmon could occasionally be seen rising to them. The flies used were artificial mayflies or 'floating flies on the principle of a mayfly, but of a somewhat stronger construction and incorporating some of the feathers which from time immemorial have been recognised material for some of the most successful salmon flies'. Ashley-Dodd also recommended up-eyed double hooks instead of singles for such flies, as giving a better hold on a hooked fish. The process of fishing was similar to that of dry-fly fishing for trout, i.e. with an upstream fly, cast on a fairly short line to a fish that preferably could be seen in the water, or at least to one whose continued rises could be spotted.

Ashley-Dodd makes two other interesting points about which he is quite definite. He emphasises that the strike should not be too quick, and says that several fish were missed in his early days of dry-fly fishing through too hurried striking. He further adds: 'A salmon for some reason closes his lips on the fly in a much more leisurely manner than a trout, and therefore he wants a slower strike'.

He also talks about the value of a dragged dry-fly for salmon: 'If you have any drag on your fly when casting over a trout—down he goes; but very often the reverse is the case when a dragged fly comes over a salmon—up he comes!'

He recounts that he once caught four salmon in one day on dry-fly, up to 22lb. in weight, a remarkable achievement surely justifying serious consideration being given to this method of fishing. Yet except on the Test, as recounted later in this chapter, no one else in this country seems ever to have devoted much attention to it.

Ashley-Dodd makes no mention of suitable water temperature in connection with the use of the dry-fly. This is a pity as one imagines it must be a factor of considerable importance. How warm should the water be before the dry-fly stands a reasonable chance of success? The water temperature of the lower Test in mayfly time usually lies between 60°–65°F, and is not likely to be colder.

Apart from Ashley-Dodd's experiences, the fishery

manager of a well known trout dry-fly fishery on the Test has recently written to me as follows: 'It is not uncommon for us to catch a few salmon each year. I can remember two salmon being caught when rising to mayfly and being caught on a mayfly, the angler using the equivalent of a 1 x cast on a 9 foot trout rod. I myself have caught two salmon on a dry-fly here in July, using ordinary trout tackle fished upstream in the usual manner, the fly on both occasions being a large Red Wulff.

I have also been present when fish have been caught on an upstream nymph, usually weighted so that, cast well in front, it will sink down and float past the salmon's face. In our clear water it is possible to see the fish open its mouth to take the nymph.

If I spot a salmon in the right sort of lie, it will often take a large dry-fly. It will almost certainly lift in the water if it does not take, and therefore show some interest. A test – then try the upstream nymph. I've been amazed how many times one or the other works. Here in mid-summer, when the water is very clear, during a day's trout fishing one often spots a salmon with the aid of polaroid glasses. It is always north a few casts with a big fly, and of course one should take the precaution of removing one's 4lb. point and getting back to something a bit stronger. Last but most important, don't strike too quickly.'

Transferring attention to the other side of the Atlantic, one finds that Colonel George La Branche was one of the earliest and most outstanding protagonists of the dry-fly for salmon in New Brunswick. He left an interesting record of his conclusions in his well known book, *The Salmon and the Dry-Fly* published in 1914. It seems that he had no great difficulty in catching Canadian salmon by this method, for example he records catching no less than 23 salmon and grilse to his own rod on the dry-fly before lunch one day on the Upsalquitch River in New Brunswick, every fish being seen before it was cast to. Such ideas by British standards can be consigned to the Never Never Land! It was a remarkable feat. In most respects La Branche agreed with Ashley-Dodd, for instance over the importance of being able to see the fish in the water, and the need for accuracy in casting, in order to float the fly *directly* over the fish. But he disagreed strongly with him over another issue, asserting that a fish will *never* rise to a dragged fly. He laid down the obvious principle that the fly should be dropped lightly on the water, a short distance immediately upstream of the fish; and that it should float high, poised on its hackle points, and downstream immediately over the fish's head. He made no mention of how quickly one should strike after a rise, but merely advised against striking too hard, in the excitement of the moment, so as to cause a break. He described the normal length of line required as being under 12 yards, from 8 yards shortest to 20 yards longest. Perhaps with modern tackle one could successfully achieve longer distances? He advocated a biggish 'palmer' type of fly, wingless, and with cock hackles tied fairly thickly, and directly at right angles to the body.

There is no doubt that La Branche succeeded in popularizing the use of the dry-fly in Canada, as opposed to the ordinary wet-fly method of long standing; and it has remained popular there to this present day. The above shows that in Canadian waters it is an effective method of fishing. It would not otherwise have survived, let alone developed to its present extent. Incidentally George La Branche came over to the Dee at Cairnton to try out the dry-fly in the Summer of 1925 on Mr Arthur Wood's water. The result was something of a fiasco. He rose around twenty fish, but only hooked two, and landed none. There is an interesting account of this episode in *Greased Line Fishing* by Jock Scott.

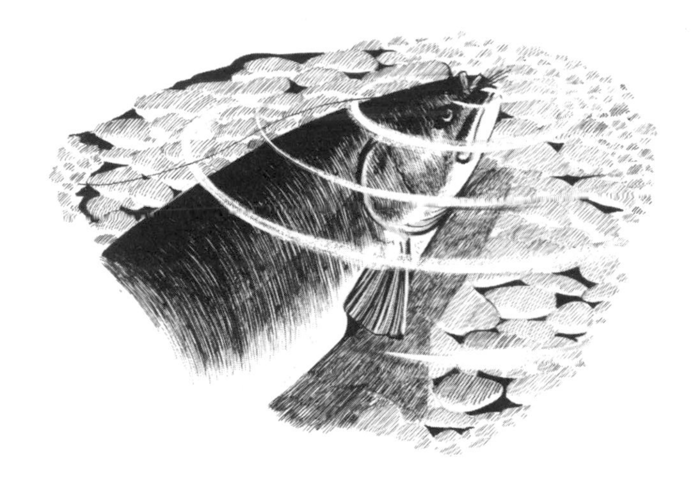

An expert American angler of the 1920s, a friend and successor to La Branche, was Mr E. R. Hewitt, who in 1922 wrote and published a detailed book, *Secrets of the Salmon*. A lengthy chapter in this book is devoted to dry-fly fishing. It is full of interesting information, and any present-day fisherman who is prepared to explore the possibilities of dry-fly should not fail to read it. Hewitt is specific about water temperatures. He says: *Salmon do not take a dry-fly well when the water is below 58°F, and begin to take it well when the water is 60°F. The best dry-fly condition is with the water 60°F to 66°F.* So here is definite and clear-cut information about water temperatures, better than can be found elsewhere.

In other ways Hewitt confirmed largely what La Branche had previously said; but he used a shorter rod of 10½ feet, and a longer line, saying that he regularly fished 70 feet (23 yards) with ease. His leader seemed often to be of 14 feet, in length, and a fine leader was preferable in bright sunlight. The dry-fly was undoubtedly superior to the wet-fly in low clear water, and the fly must pass directly over the fish. In contrast to wet-fly, which offers its best attraction when first seen (diminishing with the number of times the salmon sees it), the dry-fly increases in attractiveness with repeated presentation, even over as long a period as an hour. Hewitt also points out that a dry-fly pulled away from a fish and *below the surface* can be deadly. He says that 'under certain conditions this method takes fish better than any other'.

Mr John Rennie, a British fisherman of some standing earlier this century, has an interesting account of successful operations with the dry-fly for Icelandic salmon in his book *I Have Been Fishing*. He recounts how he and his friends went to Iceland in 1921, to a minor west-coast river which had plenty of small salmon and grilse. The weather was warm with brilliant sunshine, and the water low and clear. Ordinary greased line fishing was effective for a time, but soon the fish became shy, so other tactics had to be adopted. Rennie fell back on the dry-fly, which was at once successful, up to a point. Plenty of fish were risen but not hooked. One member of the party rose nine in one day but killed none. Rennie himself rose five in one pool the same afternoon, but apparently also failed to land one. He described this episode as follows: 'That afternoon I rose five fish in a pool, which had a high overhanging rock above it, from which one of my fishing companions was looking on. This is what was seen—the salmon rose and took the fly, but before you could count one the fly was ejected. We had all been giving plenty of time, as one does to big sea-trout and Kennet trout. So we changed our ideas and next day there was a very different story to tell. Fish rose, sometimes head and tail, sometimes a savage plunge, sometimes just a nose. We struck as quickly as we could, and to our surprise hooked the fish and landed them. This added a new lease of life to the river, and a new pleasure in salmon fishing.'

Unfortunately however there is no record in Rennie's book of the number of fish actually killed on the dry-fly in Iceland, so one is left wondering whether or not the above episode was in the nature of a flash in the pan. Rennie goes on to say that on occasion he rose salmon on the dry-fly in both Lewis and Islay, also in Norway when sea-trout fishing; but he gives no further description of dry-fly fishing among his later experiences, so it does not appear as though he persevered with it. He makes no mention of suitable water temperature, but in the west of Iceland with several days of brilliant summer sun and low water one would expect the water temperature to be around 65°F and possibly warmer. He summarizes the prospects of dry-fly fishing in Britain as follows: 'I think there is a good reason why we don't catch fish in Scotland on the dry-fly, the reason being that we hardly ever try it. My opinion is that, given very clear water, a bright day, and plenty of fish, they will rise to the dry-fly.

The fact is, when you are catching all the fish you want on greased line, you can't be bothered with experiments in dry-fly, when your time is limited to two or three weeks fishing.'

Very well then, and this reasoning seems sound enough, but again we are left wondering why Rennie did not subsequently use this method more often.

Another trans-Atlantic expert on dry-fly salmon fishing is Mr Lee Wulff, who has written a comprehensive book, *The Atlantic Salmon* first published in 1958, and now in a revised and updated edition. This book enters into great detail about both wet and dry-fly fishing, and like La Branche, Mr Wulff gives the impression that under the right conditions salmon can be caught readily in Canada on the dry-fly. As to when to use the dry-fly, here is an extract from the first edition.

> 'There is a general impression that dry-fly fishing is effective only in the late summer under warm low water conditions, and that wet flies are best when the rivers are high and cold. There is a certain truthful generality to that premise, but it is not precisely bounded. It is logical to believe that if a salmon can be drawn to within a few inches of the surface to take a wet-fly, he can also be drawn to the top for a floating fly. Experience supports this, so let us consider the use of the dry-fly and wet-fly as being roughly similar in their power to pull rises when both are fished in the conventional manner on or near the surface.'

Doubtless this recommendation is wholly valid in Canada, but how does it apply in Britain? Over here we might expect to catch fish on flies close to the surface when the water temperature rises to about 48°F (give or take a degree or two). If the weather is unusually warm and the water low and clear, the operative temperature might be 3 degrees lower. Does Mr Wulff's recommendation mean that here in Britain we could catch fish on the dry-fly with water at this temperature? This would seem to be an unlikely idea, even though admittedly the dry-fly is never tried here under such conditions. And for an odd fish that might so be caught one would have thought that scores could be taken by the more usual methods. But this may be a mistaken view . . . it would be of immense interest to have more information.

Mr Wulff's recommendations as to type of fly and manner of fishing do not differ in essentials from what La Branche advocated a generation earlier, though of course rods and reels had improved by Wulff's type, becoming lighter and more easily handled. In particular short single handed rods had come into fashion, together more recently with plastic coated lines. As to striking, Mr Wulff's recommendation is a simple one. It is that the right time to strike is 'after the fish has taken the fly into his mouth, and before he spits it out'. This is plain and straightforward advice, but possibly not quite so simple as it sounds. There may be a number of 'false rises' when the fish merely goes through the motions without actually taking the fly. To strike at these, in pent-up excitement, is likely to alarm the fish and put him down. Equally the fish, when he has taken the fly, can spit it out very quickly; so it is unwise to delay the strike too long. There is in fact a need for very precise timing in striking.

In 1976 Mr Shirley E. Woods produced an interesting book *Angling for Atlantic Salmon*. Except for one chapter on the Grimsa River in Iceland this book is entirely concerned with fishing in Canada, including Labrador. Mr

Woods, like Lee Wulff and La Branche, does not seem to rate the catching of salmon on the dry-fly as a particularly difficult process, and he goes out of his way to confirm all La Branche's first observations, about precision in casting and accuracy in floating the fly directly over the fish; but he says 'drag is not critical', and 'the correct time to strike is *after* the fly is in the salmon's mouth, but before he spits it out' (thus repeating Lee Wulff). His recommended patterns of dry-flies and of rods, tackle, and procedure also re-echo for the most part those of Lee Wulff and earlier writers.

So, in conclusion, what are we to gather from all this expert advice? The whole matter is surely one of great interest, and not less so because certain items of advice seem contradictory—e.g. the advisability or otherwise of drag, and how quick should be the strike. On the other hand there seems to be basic agreement that it is highly desirable to be able to see in the water the fish that one is aiming at, that it is preferable to fish him from fairly close downstream, i.e. twenty yards or slightly less, that it is important to float the fly *exactly* over the fish's nose, and that it may be necessary to continue casting over him time and time again before he can be induced to rise or take.

Turning to the question of a suitable type of rod, it seems that a single handed split-cane of nine to ten feet in length, or now of course in fibre-glass or carbon graphite as an alternative, is what is wanted; and the line should be a floating one, with a forward taper and of appropriate weight. The leader should be of best quality nylon monofilament, of three to four yards in length, tapered to a point of 8 to 10lb breaking strain. There should naturally be plenty of backing on the reel to allow the fish to run freely when hooked. As to striking, there seems to be a divergence of opinion, but perhaps less so than appears at first sight. It cannot be wrong for the fisherman to watch his fly intently, to refrain from striking at 'false rises', but to strike firmly and quickly the moment that the fish has actually got the fly in his mouth. It seems likely that as grilse are quicker in their reactions and movements than salmon they should be struck more quickly.

Some patterns of salmon dry-flies

Concerning flies, there seems to be general agreement also on the advisability of a fairly big well-hackled fly, that will float readily 'on the points of the tackle' when dressed with Mucilin or some similar unguent which is easily obtainable. Salmon will take an artificial mayfly at times. There are many varied Canadian patterns of suitable flies for dry-fly fishing, differing little in their main essentials . . . all thickly hackled, mostly in palmer fashion, some with hair wings and some without. Some of the best known patterns appear to be the various Wulff flies, Irresistibles, Pink Lady, Colonel Monell, and Soldier Palmer. It does not seem as though pattern makes a lot of difference, though attention should be paid to suitable sizes to be varied according to the salmon's day to day preference. There are no dry-flies of British origin suitable for salmon, except possibly variants of the mayfly.

Whether stale salmon will take a dry-fly as readily as fresh ones is not made clear; one would expect this to be in conformity with the salmon's behaviour towards other forms of fly or bait, i.e. that the fresher he is the better he takes, and vice versa. But one would like confirmation of this.

It is curious that none of the experts above, with the notable exception of Hewitt, makes fully clear the desirable water temperature for dry-fly, which one would imagine to be such an important factor. Is it taken for granted that water temperatures in Canada are normally at about 58°F or higher? (so that this point can largely be overlooked). If one follows Hewitt's advice, one is better off not to use dry-fly unless the water is at least at 58°F, and 60°F or over is better. Although such temperatures may be common in Canada, they are becoming fairly warm for Scotland, though less so for Southern England.

If one needs the presence of fresh fish in fair numbers, coupled with such temperatures, for the dry-fly to be at its best, such a combination of circumstances in years gone by did not occur any too frequently in Britain, when the best of the salmon run used to be over by June. But nowadays, with our present greatly increased run of summer salmon and grilse from the end of June onwards, it does seem to occur much more often. Might there not therefore be increased opportunities for the successful use of the dry-fly here? In undertaking any experiments in this enthralling branch of angling it would seem to be sound policy to start operations with the most favourable set of conditions as regards presence of fresh fish, water height and temperature, air temperature, and so on. If one could achieve some success in these circumstances, only then would it perhaps be worth while to extend one's activities to times when weather and water conditions were less favourable.

One thing is certain, one can never learn how to fish from books; so if you my reader care to experiment under suitable conditions with the dry-fly, it would be of the greatest interest to hear what you make of it. All the experts are in complete agreement that the thrill of rising and hooking a salmon to the dry-fly, particularly when one has a clear view of the fish in question, is second to nothing else in angling. This could be a recompense for less spectacular successes foregone, and less exciting opportunities unsought. How inspiring it would be if some real trans-Atlantic expert would come over to this side of the Atlantic and give us a full exposition and practical demonstration.

* * *

After I had completed writing the above, Doctor Wilfred Carter who is the Chairman of the International Atlantic Salmon Foundation, based on New Brunswick, has kindly introduced me to Mr H. G. Wellington of New York, whom he describes as knowing more about the use of dry-fly for Atlantic salmon than anyone else in these present times. Mr Wellington has provided a wealth of information about dry-fly fishing in Canada, though he has never used it elsewhere. He says 'We certainly had repeated instances of good dry-fly fishing in very high water and very low; in very cold weather and very hot; when the air was warmer than the water and vice versa; at all stages of the barometer and all directions of the wind'. He says he has himself caught and released over 500 fish on dry-fly on one particular river. In exceptional years he and his friends have caught many salmon on dry-fly which would not take a wet-fly.

As to suitable water temperature for a dry-fly, Mr Wellington says 'he cannot be very specific about it, except to guess that from 50°F to 65°F would include most of it. When the water becomes very warm, nothing works well, but the dry-fly works best, in early morning and late evening. In Canada during July it is not unusual to have air temperatures of 80°F. As long as the water remains cool this does not spoil the fishing. It is very worthwhile to try a dry-fly whenever it becomes difficult to take any fish on the wet.'

So here we have Mr Wellington's expert and up-to-date advice, given in unmistakably clear terms. It does not differ markedly from the previous recommendations in this chapter, but we learn that in Canada at any rate the dry-fly can be effective under a variety of different weather and water conditions. It is also the best method when conditions are 'very warm'.

July in Canada 'not unusually' provides an air temperature of 80°F, also that dry-fly is effective there at any water temperature from about 50°F to 65°F. The only point where Mr Wellington's advice does not seem completely clear-cut in fact concerns the most favourable water temperature. But all in all, when we consider his remarks, together with those of the other experts above, it seems we cannot be wrong if we assume that any water temperature from say 58°F (thus making allowance for any uncertainty), to 65°F or slightly higher would be suitable for dry-fly.

In addition to the above, I have now received further detailed information from Mr Shirley E. Woods, the expert dry-fly fisherman mentioned earlier in this chapter. The important feature in this information is that Mr Woods confirms definitely that the appropriate water temperature for the use of the dry-fly is 58°F or warmer. He also makes the interesting point that it often pays 'to cast to a single fish from a point roughly opposite the lie. This strategy keeps the amount of slack line to a minimum and ensures that only the fly and leader pass over the salmon.' In other ways Mr Woods largely confirms what has already been recommended in this chapter.

14
Wading

Wading is an infernal nuisance, except on a very hot day when one can cool off in the water . . . there is little doubt about that. It is slow, irksome, tiring, distracting, plus any other opprobrious descriptives which you like to attach to it. It can be dangerous for those who cannot swim, and even for those who can. What a relief it is to fish on a river like the Test, Avon, or Frome where little or no wading is necessary! If one set out to devise the most impossible, uncomfortable, and unsuitable garment for hot weather, it would be hard to beat a pair of long trouser waders with heavy brogues (though they could be an asset on a pouring wet day, or when the spring or autumn wind blows cold).

On the other hand wading is an integral and essential part of the process of salmon fishing on almost all rivers, especially the north-country ones. If one cannot wade (and there are not a few who for varying reasons can't), one is confined to boat or bank fishing, and is therefore largely out of the game. If one wants to be an all-round fisherman who can put up a fair performance on any type of water, it is surely worthwhile therefore giving close consideration to wading and all that goes with it. I am skipping the elementary principles such as not transferring weight to the forward foot until the new foothold is secure, not trying to progress through the water too quickly, not wading too far onto gravel spits with deep water all round, and not standing on submerged rocks, again with deep water all round—all these are important, but I am sure my readers are already sufficiently acquainted with them.

The main purpose of wading it need hardly be said is to enable one to fish fly or bait over the salmon in an effective manner. Other subsidiary objects may also be taken into account, such as wading out into the river to clear the line from some obstruction or to play a fish on a shorter line than from the bank (thus avoiding being 'drowned'). Also, if no bridge or boat is available and one wants to cross to the other bank for some purpose or other, one can wade right across a river that is not too deep.

Wading is not an end in itself, as sometimes seems to be imagined. Even in a big river there is no need to wade in a foot further than is strictly necessary to cover the fish in a workmanlike manner. I once knew a Spey fisherman who prided himself on invariably wading to the very top inch of his trouser waders. It was an astonishing exhibition, and how unnecessary and indeed detrimental! His fly would not have fished properly, if at all, over all the fish lying close in on the near side of any stream which he fished; and as he went down the pool he would have disturbed all such fish from their lie, not helpful for any angler following him. In most pools some of the fish are almost certain to be lying on the near side of the main current, and in a wide river it may be worthwhile fishing any pool twice, provided time allows, wading in only a short distance first time down to cover the nearer fish properly, and as deeply as possible second time down, to cover the outliers.

In general the fly or bait when cast should land in the

water, so far as is humanly possible, well beyond and not on top of the lie of the fish. The angler should wade in just so far and no further than allows him to achieve this result, and allows him to fish his fly or bait round at the right speed (not too fast) over the fish. So there is no hard and fast rule about how far he should wade in, and he must estimate this for himself. An underestimate or an overestimate are both serious errors. As a general rule it is better to rely on the principle of wading in only a comparatively short distance and compensating for this by using a long line, rather than the opposite; but each individual must judge for himself what he can do best, according to his capability. Also the set of the current differs in different pools, so what is appropriate in one place may not be so in another. There are no fixed rules of procedure in this, no more than in many other aspects of fishing.

One thing however is definitely a good principle, and that is that the wader should be able to swim! It is not difficult to swim in waders, anyhow for a short distance. I have done it twice myself, so know this for a fact. If the wader knows he can swim should he be so unfortunate as to get washed out of his depth, it gives him an innate confidence at all times which would otherwise be lacking, and it may possibly save him from drowning into the bargain. So this should not be overlooked. In addition it greatly helps if he has learnt to wade when young. I known in my own case that I started wading in the Aberdeenshire Dee at the age of nine in rubber soled thigh boots, which became by degrees more treacherous and more slippery on a rough bottom. It was good training for the future, and I have never found any difficulty in wading anywhere since those early days. Rubber soles by the way are a deplorable form of footwear for any waders. As they wear smooth they become suicidally slippery on stones or rock. Avoid them like the plague! Going back to the advisability of learning to wade well when one is young, like most other achievements it seems much easier then. I have known those who have taken up wading in middle age never being at ease with it.

Two points about deep wading are perhaps worth noting. The first is that it takes a lot of weight off the legs, and so is less tiring (provided the current is not unduly strong). If you are wading waist deep the weight of the lower half of your body is naturally borne by the water. The second is that you are probably less likely to fall in when wading deep, because you will be supported to a certain extent by the water all round you from the waist down, also you will probably wade with extra caution and will have to progress slowly. Knee-deep is often the most dangerous depth, especially when coupled with undue haste or if the wader is tired after a long day's fishing. If you do fall in while wading, you may curse and swear as much as you like which won't do any harm, but don't worry too much! It happens to all of us. The best course is to kneel on the bottom if you can do so and keep your head above water at the same time, facing upstream, and get up very slowly and deliberately so as to avoid falling in a second time. If you get out of your depth and have to swim for it, head for the nearest bit of shallow water or bank in a downstream direction. Keep hold of your rod if you can do so. It is annoying to fall in, but even more annoying to lose your rod, reel, and line as well. If you can't swim and are out of your depth, it would seem you are much more poorly placed! and I am doubtful what advice to give. I am told that if you lie on your back in the water you will float for a certain length of time and can with luck paddle yourself to within reach of a rock that you can cling to or else into shallow water. I know two ghillies neither of whom can swim, one on the Spey and one on the Tweed, who were washed out of their depth and saved themselves in this way. Both survived, but it must have been an unnerving experience, which is why I say it must undoubtedly be better to know how to swim.

All waders (garments) are uncomfortable, but some less so than others, which is the best that can be said about them. Whether you use a pair with boots attached, 'all in one', or a pair that need separate socks and brogues is up to you. Both have their merits and drawbacks. For many years now I have used a series of light rubber waders, milk-chocolate in colour, which are long and enable me to go in deep if I want to. They need socks and brogues, and I have some special light-weight felt-soled patterns of the latter, which are as comfortable as any brogues can be. This outfit has done me very well; it is light for walking and the waders if punctured can be quickly and readily patched. On the other hand they let in the cold easily; one needs plenty of room inside them for lots of warm clothes in spring and autumn, though this is an essential in waders of any kind for that matter. There are however now many types of waders of different sorts on the market, and there is not a lot to choose between the better patterns. As to the type of sole, this again is a matter of personal preference. Leather soles heavily nailed are good until the nails wear smooth, which they do before long, and then they become slippery. Felt for soles is comfortable and gives a good foothold but wears through quickly. Perhaps the best combination is to have felt soles of double thickness and nailed leather heels. Such soles last a fair time, and the heels can easily be re-nailed.

Whether you use a wading stick or not is again a matter of personal choice, also of experience and age. If you are young and agile you can most probably dispense with one, unless in unknown and particularly difficult water. As you get older you will find a wading stick a considerable asset, particularly if your sense of balance begins to deteriorate. It is a sensible idea to combine a wading staff and long handled gaff. Don't forget however that once you have become used to a wading stick, you will find it difficult to dispense with one. One point which I think is worth emphasizing is that, if you are wading in a really strong current in a big water like the Spey or Dee, and you begin to feel unsure of your foothold having ventured too far in a strong stream, on no account attempt to turn round, presenting in doing so your face or back to the current. If you do this you will expose a bigger area of your body to the force of the water pressure, and may well be swept off your feet. The right course in these circumstances is to edge sideways downstream, gradually inching back into quieter water. Use the butt of your rod as an emergency wading staff if you are in real trouble, and as you move inwards and downstream you should find the water pressure easing.

Accidents or duckings usually happen not in the obviously hazardous places, where everyone takes great care, but in the harmless looking places which do not have any appearance of danger to those who do not know them well. One of the most dangerous places of this type which I know of is on the lower Tay. On the left bank there is a gravelly shallow, and the fish lie perhaps 65 yards out from the edge of the river in a deep trough. As you wade out the river slowly increases in depth from ankle to knee deep, but when you are 40 yards out there is still no depth to it, though the stream is gradually increasing. You can see the fish jumping, still well beyond your reach, so you proceed further. By the time you are up to your fork you can probably cover the nearest of the fish, but the stream by now is unpleasantly strong, you can only just stand against it, and the loose gravel bottom is treacherously unstable underfoot. Being now almost in the middle of the river you start to wade on downstream, to cover as much water as possible, but there is a horrible trap only a short distance away in the form of a sudden and steep descent into water fifteen or so feet deep and below it a vast whirly-hole. A really forbidding place, made worse by the gravel giving way under your feet if you go too near the edge of the deep.

If you did go in out of your depth in this place you would be in real trouble, and I know of two unfortunate anglers who have in fact been drowned here in recent years. This is typical of the sort of place I am trying to describe, which looks harmless but can be a killer. Such places are made worse if the angler who tries to wade them is tired after a long day's fishing. In such circumstances extra care should without doubt be taken.

While on the subject of risks involved in wading there is one particular one which should be drawn to the reader's attention, and that is the danger of cramp. To have a sudden attack of cramp while far out in the river is a most unpleasant experience. One immediate antidote to cramp is salt. If therefore the angler is addicted to sudden attacks of cramp, it is a wise precaution for him to carry in his pocket a small tin of salt tablets. The wearing of waders for long periods at a time in hot weather brings out the sweat in large quantities. This in turn leads to cramp, which often seems to be a salmon fisherman's occupational malady.

There is one piece of good advice about wading which I am sure I should mention before closing this chapter, and that is to keep moving briskly onwards when fishing down a long pool. It is very easy for a fisherman who is nervous of his foothold and uncertain of the river bed to fall into the trap of taking two or three casts at every wading stance before steeling himself to move on again. This leads to unnecessary delay, greatly restricting the amount of water that can be covered in a day's fishing, and aggravating for anyone else who may be waiting to follow him down a pool. Novices in wading are particularly liable to indulge in such hesitation. The competent fisherman by contrast should keep wading boldly onwards, with two or three good steps between each cast, and only slowing up if he has reached a particularly likely taking place, or if he has risen or pulled a fish. An alternative system which can be adopted is for the angler to start casting with a short line and make four or five casts standing in the same place but lengthening the line by a yard or two at each cast until he is throwing his maximum length. He then wades down eight or ten yards, and goes through the same process; and so on until the length of the pool is covered. There is something to be said for this method. It is less laborious and presents the fly at different angles to the fish, though it probably takes up more time.

15
Boat Fishing

Boat fishing is necessary in many though not all of the pools on big rivers, if the water is to be properly covered. I have in mind such rivers as the Tay, Spey and Tweed; and also the big rivers of Norway. If the fish are lying far out from the bank, where the water is too deep to enable the angler to cover them by wading, a boat preferably with a good boatman is a sine qua non.

On the biggest rivers of all, such as the Tana, Mals, Vefsen, and Namsen amongst others in Norway, and the Tay in Scotland, recourse is often had to harling with an outboard motor. This is an exceptionally dull form of fishing, so it seems to me, and I would not advise any of my readers to try it. It involves traversing the river under power from an outboard motor to and fro across the lies of the fish, with two or three rods trailing different lengths of line from the stern of the boat, and with lures of different types at the end of a strong leader attached to each line. All that the angler has to do is to see that his lures are working properly, i.e. that they fish at the right depth, and do not get intertangled, fouled by weed or leaves, or catch the bottom. When a fish takes he will hook himself or not as the case may be; and the angler has only to hold on hard and land the fish in the quickest time possible on the strong tackle employed, so as to restart the process as quickly as he can.

Casting from an anchored boat is an easy method of

fishing, in the sense of being less tiring and involving less hard work for the fisherman. He need not have to don long waders, for instance, as thigh waders or even gumboots will be adequate. He avoids the labour of wading deep in what in most places is likely to be a strong stream, and of immersing himself in water which in spring or autumn at any rate is bound to be unpleasantly cold. What is more the boat can probably be manoeuvred to enable him to cover the fish more effectively and with a shorter line. It may well transport him more easily and quickly from pool to pool, thus saving a lot of walking. It will lose no time in taking him across the river, if he wants to fish from the opposite side; and it helps in playing a large and active fish that runs out a long line in a strong and wide pool. The fish can if necessary be followed, so as to avoid the line being snagged or drowned; and if in spite of all it does get snagged, the boat can be used to release it, the fish with luck being still on the end. Lastly the fisherman will have the company of a boatman, who will not only shoulder the burden of boat management but will land the fish for him with net or gaff, and whose advice where to fish is likely to be highly valuable. He may further get a fund of racy local stories if the boatman is an affable and conversational character, as most of them are. I never yet, personally, met a ghillie or boatman whose company I disliked; irritating just occasionally perhaps, but interesting always. Fishing would lose a great deal through their absence.

Some people say that they dislike the use of boats. I never could understand this, unless it was that they preferred to fish alone, and were embarrassed by the presence of a boatman. No one admittedly would want to fish from boats all the time, even on a big river; and in some places and particularly in time of medium and low water one definitely does better wading. On all the three Scottish rivers mentioned above there are endless small 'neuks', minor streams and catches, and deep holding places close under the bank where the use of a boat would be superfluous and time wasting. Such places can probably be fished in ten minutes or so by wading or off the bank, if no offer is obtained; and yet be prolific on occasion. The wading fisherman can move quickly from one to the next as he judges it advantageous, in fact the boat as a general rule is an asset for fishing the larger pools only.

It could also be argued that there is a good deal to be said for independence in fishing—to pit one's wits single-handed against the fish, and to beat him or be beaten by him alone and without outside help. For example the crowning ambition of a salmon fisherman's career might be envisaged as the capture of a 50 or even 40 pounder by the fisherman on his own and without the help of a ghillie. How much greater must be this achievement if it is single-handed; and I know two fisherman who in the case of a 50 pounder have been successful in exactly this way. One could indeed be envious! One is Major Anthony Tabor, and the other Major Richard Waddington, and the scene of their triumph was on the Rauma and Aaro respectively.

To return to the subject of boat fishing, to have a boat available for use as an alternative to wading or bank fishing, when and where wanted, always seems to me to be a decided advantage on any large river; and this even if no boatman is available, and one has to run it oneself with a rope and anchor, (not difficult if one knows how.).

Each river is apt to have a different type of boat and a different method of working it. The Tay has big cobles, stable and strongly built, that will hold four people if necessary, the boatman and three passengers—though a total complement of three is more suitable. Power is provided by an outboard motor that will make headway upstream through any rapid, and a pair of oars together with a long rope and 56lb anchor weight are part of the equipment. Apart from harling, boat fishing in the Tay is carried out by casting, with the boat riding at anchor in a suitable position and the boatman gradually letting out rope so that as much water as possible is covered before the need occurs to up-anchor and move on.

Tay boat, 16 ft 6 in long.

If a fish is hooked there are three possible courses, one is for it to be landed into the boat. This entails playing it from the boat, then ottering the boat so far as possible into quiet water, and when the fish is tired the angler seated near the bow runs it on a short line close up to the stern where the boatman can either net or gaff it into the boat. Boatmen are rather apt to favour this method with small fish of about 10lb or less, because it saves them the trouble of taking the boat into the side. Provided the fish is firmly hooked all normally goes well; but lightly hooked fish and grilse are lost in a bigger proportion than if played in the orthodox way from near or on the bank. It is therefore basically an unsound method.

The second possible procedure is for the boatman as soon as possible after the fish is hooked to pull the boat up to the anchor, hoist the anchor aboard, and row to the bank, or to quiet water near the bank, and land the fish there. This is a sound course, but it does of course entail more effort for the boatman, especially if frequently repeated.

The third course is a modification of the second one. If every 20 yards or so on the anchor rope there is a quick release clip, and if a small buoy such as a corked and empty plastic container is kept in the boat, which can quickly be attached to the loose end of the anchor rope when the clip is released, the anchor attached to the now buoyed rope can be abandoned, as soon as a fish is hooked, and the boat being freed can be rowed to the bank or quiet water. This last is the best system of all, and when the fish has been either landed or lost the boat can be rowed out or taken out under half throttle again to pick up the buoyed end of the anchor rope so that fishing can continue. Needless to say if a big fish is hooked it is really essential to adopt the second or third method above.

The procedure on the Spey is rather different. The normal Spey boat is smaller than its Tay counterpart, and will not take a total of more than two people with comfort.

It needs however to be strongly built to compete with the many rocks in the river bed and along the banks, and with the strong Spey current. The method of working it is usually by rope and anchor, that is to say a rope of some 80 to 100 yards in length, wound from side to side across the boat on cleats, and attached to an anchor in the form of a 56lb weight or a three or four pronged iron pattern with flukes. The weight is the more secure version, but is heavy to lift up into the boat. The pronged anchor is lighter, and therefore easier to handle, but can get jammed amongst scattered rocks on the river bottom. So both types have their advantages and drawbacks.

Spey boat, 14 ft long.

The method of working the boat to fish a pool is as follows. The boatman rows the boat out to the appropriate place near the neck of the pool, and drops the anchor just out of the main stream. Having then let out a few yards of rope he can steady the boat, with the two oars suspended in the water on thole pins. The oars play an important part in acting as a rudder and preventing the boat from 'yawing'. They should hang on the outside of the thole pins, not on the inside in the position one would have them for rowing. They are liable occasionally to jump off the pins and fall into the river, so it is as well to have them tied to the boat with a length of cord, also to carry a third spare oar in the boat in case of one of the oars in use breaking.

Once he has got both anchor and boat properly positioned according to the line on which he wants to descend down the pool, the boatman lets out the rope a yard or so at a time, while his fisherman is casting. In this way the pool can be fished down for the whole length of the rope. When all the rope is out, and if the full length of the pool is still not covered, the boatman pulls the boat up to the anchor, hauls it on board, and drops down to a fresh anchorage below until the tail of the pool is reached.

When a fish is hooked it is seldom necessary for the boatman to go through the elaborate process of pulling up to the anchor and hoisting it aboard. With a fair length of rope out he can almost always otter inshore by transferring the rope to the outside cleat, thus turning the bow towards the bank. He can use the oars to help the process if necessary, and deposit the fisherman into shallow water or directly onto the bank to play the fish from there. This procedure is usually easier on the Spey than on the Tay, because although faster it is a narrower river, and the boat is seldom anchored far out from the bank.

This system works well, though it makes it necessary to have a separate boat on every pool which is to be fished in this way. Spey rapids are very strong and rocky; it is doubtful whether an outboard motor could be successfully used to take a boat upstream through them, and in any case outboard motors are never used on this river. There are of course some drawbacks to the method, as might be expected. One is that a strong crosswind makes the boat 'yaw' badly from side to side, while an upstream wind can make it difficult to get the boat to drop down. In either case a drogue, (an old bucket will do if nothing better is available), attached to the stern and suspended in the stream can be a great help. A dragging anchor is another menace. If the boat is anchored too far out in a strong stream the anchor may start to drag. If it does, the best thing is at once to pull the boat up to it (or to pull it down to the boat), hoist it aboard, and row to the shore to start the whole process again, anchoring nearer in next time. If the boat is allowed to be drawn down into a rapid with the anchor still out, the latter will almost certainly jam behind a rock, and the bow will at once be pulled right under by the fierce rush of the stream. Any immediate likelihood of this happening should be countered at once by a quick severing of the anchor rope, and the boat guided down the rapid by use of the oars. The severed rope and anchor can be recovered later by one means or another.

Another possible contretemps arising from the use of an anchored boat is if, while a fish is being played from it, he runs upstream and under the rope. There is an immediate and effective answer to this, which is to pass the rod over the stern with its point near water level, guide the line under the boat in the same direction as the fish has passed under the rope, and all will be well!—that is unless the fish has run back once more under the rope, in which case the action should be repeated in the opposite direction. If a cool head is kept in such crises there should usually be no difficulty.

Before leaving the subject of Spey boats there is one further small point which should be noted, that is the easiest way for the angler to get out of them in order to get to the bank when playing a fish. This is to sit on the stern facing downstream and drop off feet first into shallow water. This is a quick and shipshape form of exit, avoiding any possibility of tripping over oars, rope, or gunwale, or any other clumsiness of this sort. It should not be forgotten.

One other method of letting down a Spey boat which is occasionally used is for the ghillie to stand on the bank or wade a short distance into the water, and otter the boat downstream on a long cord attached to the nearside cleat, with the fisherman casting from the boat. This too is a system which can work quite well at times when the set of the current is right, though a strong wind can make it difficult. When a fish is hooked the ghillie simply pulls the boat straight to the bank, this process being helped if the fisherman lifts the cord off the cleat.

An energetic and willing ghillie, if particularly devoted to his 'rod', will sometimes wade into the river up to waist deep, and hold the boat in position while fishing is carried on. He can wade down the pool, holding the boat all the time (if he is willing to do so!). But to my mind this is asking too much of a ghillie.

Turning southwards to the Tweed, here an entirely different system of boat control is the usual modus operandi. The boats, to start with, are built more lightly, are more manoeuvrable, and draw less water. They are not suitable for holding more than two people, boatman and angler, and have a revolving seat after the fashion of a piano stool

Tweed boat, 13 ft long

in the stern for the benefit of the angler. The boatman prefers to row, or rather paddle, the whole time (it may be for the whole day), both while the angler is fishing and when the boat is being manoeuvred into position or across the river. The advantages of this system are many—a skilled boatman will always have his boat correctly positioned so that the water is covered in the most effective way; there is no long anchor rope out which may serve to frighten fish from returning to their lies once the boat has passed downstream and past them; there is no loss of time in changing the position of the boat while fishing is in progress or in crossing the river when necessary; lastly a pool can be 'backed up', which is sometimes a most killing procedure. This is effective chiefly on a long 'dub', or slack stretch of slow running water, which is holding fish but lacks current. The boat is dropped to the tail of the pool, and is then rowed very slowly upstream and to one side of the lie of the fish, the fisherman casting square across and over the fish as he goes. The upstream movement of the boat draws the fly over and across the fish until the line straightens out below the boat. This sytem is wrong in theory as the thick dressed line and the nylon cast both pass over the fish before they see the fly. However practice and theory in this, as in many other things in life, are two different things! In fact this method works well, and many fish are caught by it which would otherwise not be tempted. It is effective even in a flat calm, though is better still with a good ripple on the water. An upstream wind is best for producing the latter.

It might be thought that the system of perpetual rowing was a tiring one for the boatman. So it is, but usually much less so than might be expected. In normal circumstances there is very little effort needed in paddling with the oars to produce the required steadying effect. The boats as already mentioned are very light and shallow in draught, while the Tweed current on average runs at less than half the speed of that of the Spey. It is quite a different matter however with a strong downstream wind. Then as can be imagined it can be a back-breaking job for the boatman to hold his boat anywhere near steady. A strong current does not help. Some boatmen try putting out a brick on a cord or some light anchor from the bow to drag along the bottom of the river and act as a brake. This is effective until it snags fast behind a rock or in some similar obstruction, which it does frequently. The process of freeing it is tiresome and timewasting, so this too is not a fault-free answer.

As well as a downstream wind, a strong upstream wind can make matters both tiresome and laborious. It can make it very difficult for the boatman to drop the boat downstream, without a strong current to help him. A crosswind too can be tricky. A drogue would be an effective counter in both cases, but I have never known a Tweed boatman use one. The only other method of boat control which is sometimes used on the Tweed is that of ottering the boat outwards and downwards on a long line from the bank, which I have already described above in the case of the Spey. This on the Tweed too is an effective method, provided the set of the current is right and the wind not too impossible.

In passing it may be of interest to note that the style and construction of Tweed boats seem to date from long ago. For instance the famous picture of 'Rob o' the Trows' painted by R. Frain about the year 1825 shows a boat in the near background of almost identical appearance to that of modern Tweed boats. The only recent innovation is that fibre glass is now sometimes substituted for wood as construction material. It is tough, light, and resilient, long lasting and needing little maintenance, while wooden boats need painting and overhaul every year. But many boatmen still prefer wooden boats.

The only other method of boat control which I have seen practised was on the Cork Blackwater in Ireland, where the boatman let down a heavy weight on a chain attached to the bow of the boat. He then poled or paddled the boat downstream, the weight dragging along the bottom and acting as a brake while the fisherman cast from the stern. This sytem worked reasonably well with a competent boatman in charge; but again it had the drawback that the dragged weight constantly became hitched up in sunken obstructions, and time and effort was consumed in releasing it. It was not the best of systems, and it too suffered from a high wind.

A skilled waterman can operate and fish from a boat single-handed, if the boat is not too heavy, and is fitted out in the Spey fashion with cleats, rope, and anchor. This is good fun and leads to many adventures. The fish has to be played from the boat unless one can otter near enough to the bank to disembark. In the Spey one usually can, but in the Tay seldom so the fish has to be landed into the boat either by net or gaff. It is none too easy, and inevitably in the latter case one loses a certain number of fish which would otherwise have been landed; but this is all in the game.

I have often heard it discussed to what extent boats frighten fish and have a disadvantage from this angle. This is an interesting subject for investigation. The passage of a boat close to a fish certainly does not terrify him, as would a seal or an otter or for that matter a net. It does however move him out of his lie if it is close enough, and he will not return to it as long as the boat (or an anchor rope) remains close at hand. How near can a boat approach before a fish loses his nerve and swims away? This varies, there is no hard and fast rule. The deeper the water the closer he will allow the boat to come, but if the fisherman in the boat stands up and waves a long rod energetically, needless to say he will move off sooner. If the stream is strong and the surface ruffled on the other hand, it may be possible to bring the boat quite close to him. As a general estimate it might be said that seven yards or thereabouts is the crucial distance—nearer than this, and he will probably move off, further and he will stick it out even if he sees the boat. It follows that to stand up when fishing from a boat is undesirable, and it is better to fish sitting if you can throw a good line doing so. It is also less tiring, and gives the wind less of a hold on the boat (there is less of your body offering wind-resistance). It is also safer, in that you are less likely to go overboard, a by no means unheard of contingency!

One thing is certain, in a big river like the Tay, fish as a rule will soon return to their lies after a boat has passed over them. Within a few minutes they will be jumping again in their usual places. In rivers of lesser size like the Spey this is not so certain, or rather it takes longer. If a boat had passed over the neck of a Spey pool frightening the fish out of it, I would like to give it half an hour's rest at least before I felt confident that at least some of them would have returned. They *would* return, but it would be a question of 'when'.

The smaller the river undoubtedly the more marked the disturbance created by a boat. In a small river of Naver size for instance the passage of a boat might empty the pool for a day. In addition the question of repeated boat passages has to be taken into account; in simple language, one boat passing over a big pool in a sizeable river once every day, for example, will do virtually no harm; but if a fresh boat passes over every ten minutes or so throughout the day fishing will be brought pretty well to a stop. The deduction is simple and obvious, and it all amounts to a question of degree.

This leads to the vexed question of canoeing on salmon rivers and the harm ensuing from it. Undoubtedly it would be possible for a series of canoes to pass down a sizeable salmon river without disturbing the fish at all; canoers could avoid all the salmon lies without much difficulty if they knew where to look for them. As it is however they do not apparently possess the necessary knowledge or are ever likely to do so. Again in my opinion it is a question of degree. A team of say 10 canoes passing over a pool once during a day will certainly disturb most of the fish out of their lies for the time being, and the wider the canoes are scattered the greater the number of fish likely to be disturbed.

If however this only happens once during a day, no great harm is done—very little in a river as big as the Tay, though more so in the Spey, and increasingly as the size of the river diminishes. If the feelings of a fisherman are any guide, I would be quite happy to fish a Tay pool say 10 minutes after such an event, a Spey pool after say 30 minutes, and a pool in a smaller river such as the Dee after about 40 minutes. After such an interval I would not reckon my chances impaired to any extent (though of course I could not be completely certain either way).

But this whole situation is completely altered as soon as the procession of canoes becomes anything approaching continuous or even intermittent. Canoes every morning and evening would do much harm, canoes every hour or so would be a great deal worse, till the situation for the fisherman could become impossible. It does not require much imagination to visualize the impasse. It would be made worse if canoes, instead of passing straight through a pool, circled round it for some minutes practising their manoeuvres. The present situation over this canoeing question is disquieting, and one can only hope that in the future it will be resolved satisfactorily in one way or another.

One other form of boat fishing undoubtedly deserves mention, and that is boat fishing on lochs. I should make it clear right from the start that I have had no great experience of this. I have paid four or five visits to the Grimersta, thanks to the kindness of Colonel George Kidston-Montgomerie, and I suppose the loch fishing there is as good as anywhere; but I have never been lucky enough to find the Grimersta lochs in good fishing order and well stocked with fish. So I am little more than a beginner at this form of fishing, and have no pretentions to be otherwise. I have heard it said that the sight of a salmon rising through the waves of a loch to take a fly is a thrill equal to anything else in fishing. This may well be so; but once hooked the play of the fish in still water, where there are no streams and no obstructions (except possibly weeds), and where the fish can be followed in the boat everywhere he runs, surely lacks drama. On the Grimersta too the fish are small, normally of less than 10lb; it is useless to hope for 20 or 30 pounders, and even 15lb is an exceptionally heavy weight.

Nor is the process of fishing difficult. Fly fishing for salmon on a loch is very like fishing for brown trout or sea-trout, except for the stronger tackle and longer rod normally used. Personally I prefer a rod of 12 or 13 feet, especially when carbon graphite rods are so light. A rod of this length gives greater control of line and fly and makes it easier to work the fly. A wind, with consequent ripple or wave, is a pressing need, and the boat is allowed to drift with it, the rod(s) in the boat casting as the boat drifts downwind. A drogue (sea-anchor) can be useful to slow down the speed of drift when the wind is strong. Obviously success is largely dependent on the boatman, who in the first place takes the boat to the best fishing ground, and subsequently controls it in such a way as to give his rods the best possible chance. It would make the whole process more interesting if the rods themselves (there are usually two of them per boat) were able to run the boat, had to judge for themselves the best fishing ground, and in fact were dependent on themselves alone; but on the Grimersta at any rate this is not allowed.

In time of flat calm on a loch there is very little to be done. Normal methods of fishing become virtually useless, though you can try a dry fly if you like; it has been known to work. Trolling may produce a fish or two, but it is a distasteful way of fishing. It is best to try where an inlet or outlet stream produces some sort of flow, or else to abandon fishing altogether until a breeze arrives.

Fish in a loch usually tend to gather near to the downwind shore, or where there is an inlet or outlet stream; and this is where they should be sought. Two flies of size 6 to 8 are normally used, not more for fear of tangles, and the angler should cast in a generally downwind direction, varying the angle of his delivery so that as much water as possible is covered. It is not necessary to use a long line—20 yards is ample. After the flies have lighted on the water, a moment or two should be allowed for them to sink and they should then be worked back towards the boat, the rod point being gradually raised and the line drawn in. The speed with which the flies should be worked through the water depends largely on the size of the ripple or wave—if the ripple is small quite quickly, but slower as the wave increases. A strike should quickly be made if a fish is seen to rise anywhere in the vicinity of the flies, or if the line is seen to start drawing. Here is the contrast with river fishing. In still water if no action is taken the salmon will soon spit out the fly. As to pattern or colour of fly, this appears to matter little. All the hair winged flies are good, so are shrimp flies—the only types to avoid are those with too thick a dressing. Black is as good a colour as any. During recent years on the Grimersta there has grown up a fashion of using the fly known as the 'Elverine', with its conspicuous wing feather, blue and white, from the Vulturine Guinea Fowl. It is supposed to represent a young elver, though if the salmon see any mutual resemblance I should be surprised. A longish tuft of polar bear hair or even a thin strip of polythene would appear to resemble an elver far more closely. However all that matters is whether or not the salmon take these flies, which they do quite frequently, not only on the Grimersta but in Iceland and on the Spey, Hampshire Avon, and Tay as well, as I know from personal experience. I have no doubt such flies would kill anywhere, but not better than many other good patterns.

The five Grimersta lochs are shallow and provide excellent holding water for fish. Loch Naver in Sutherland which is 6 miles long by ½ mile wide is another first class fishing ground with an average depth of about 12 feet. This loch too provides good fly fishing. Many other lochs holding salmon are to be found on the west or north coast of Scotland and in the Hebrides. There are too many to be listed here, but Loch Hope, Loch Stack, Loch Shiel, Loch Maree, and Loch Achnamoine at the head of the Helmsdale are some of the best of them. Loch Ness and Loch Tay are usually fished by trolling, one of the dullest of all methods of fishing one would have thought, which even the chance of a big fish must do little to enliven. Loch Lomond, beloved by Ian Wood, is another large sheet of water holding salmon, but here apparently a fly is often effective. The artificial Loch Faskally, close to Pitlochry, now also produces a fair number of fish. All these lochs are better fished by boat than off the bank, and needless to say all need a fair stock of fish if the fishing is to be of interest. There is nothing duller than fishing a fishless loch, which is a good deal worse than a fishless river!

There is however one marked advantage of loch fishing, and that relates to finance. It is usually far less costly fishing on a loch than fishing on a river, a factor which may well be of importance.

For myself, however, I know I am not a keen loch fisherman and would opt for a river every time. I think most of my fellow salmon fishers would agree with me; but for those who don't (or even for those who do) I would recommend two excellent books, *My Way with Salmon* by Ian Wood, which relates chiefly to Loch Lomond, and *Salmon and Trout Fishing Up to Date* by Jock Scott, which has some first class chapters on loch fishing.

16
Riverside Repairs

Mishaps to one's gear inevitably occur from time to time when one is fishing. It is as well to be prepared for these, and to have handy the necessary kit to deal with them; otherwise the best of a good day's fishing may be lost.

Leaking waders are the most usual form of trouble. If the rubber or plastic is thoroughly perished there is of course nothing to be done in remedy; and only a second pair, kept in the car or in the fishing hut, will save the situation. But if the leak is a minor one, it can probably be quickly repaired, provided some rubber patching material and strong waterproof adhesive is included in one's kit. It is essential to dry thoroughly the part of the waders affected, otherwise the adhesive will not hold; but if the sun is shining brightly, or if there is a warm fire in the hut, this should present no great problem. It is a wise precaution to patch the leak *both* sides, outside and inside, rather than on one side alone. It only takes a little longer, and increases the likelihood of the mend being waterproof. If no patching material or adhesive is available, two pieces of plastic sticking tape, affixed crosswise over the leak, and as always on both sides, may be temporarily effective; but again there should be a thorough drying of the affected area before the tape will stick fast. Should the leak be in the foot, and a large one, it may be that no effort at patching will be leak-proof. In this case, provided the water is not too cold, it may be temporarily tolerable to bind some string or sticking plaster round the outside of the wader leg above the ankle, thus stopping the water seeping up one's leg, though at the expense of a wet foot.

Breaks in rods occur not infrequently. There is always a possibility of this happening, particularly on windy days. The best remedy again is the simple one of never going fishing without taking a spare rod. But how few fishermen take the trouble to observe this elementary precaution! Riverside repairs to broken rods are usually possible however, at least to a sufficient extent to last out the remainder of the day. Two essentials are necessary, a sharp knife and a supply of plastic sticking tape, which the angler should never fail to carry with him; It also makes good sense to remember to include in your kit some strong waterproof adhesive. A greenheart rod can be quickly spliced after a rough and ready operation using knife and tape, provided the break is a slanting one. Split-cane rods present greater difficulty. If they are not broken clean through, but only weakened by one or two segments of cane giving way, it may be possible with the aid of the tape to splice in some piece of outside material, such as a short section of fence wire, or a piece of flat spring, or even a short length of sapling, to give enough backbone to the weakened section to last for the rest of the day. If the break is a clean fracture directly through a section of the rod, the only hope is to make a rough and ready splice, using the tape, with an overlap of not less than fourteen inches—such a repair will no doubt be clumsy, will shorten the rod, and will not last for long; nevertheless it may see out the rest of the day's fishing. A fisherman of foresight will always bear in mind the possibility of a rod breaking unexpectedly, and be prepared to overcome this disaster in one way or another, should it happen. How maddening to be put off the river by a broken rod on a day when the fish are taking really well! As noted above, a second rod always carried with one is the readiest answer to this calamitous predicament.

A broken reel spring, nullifying the check, is always also a possibility. Some of the best quality reels carry a spare spring fitted inside them, in which case a remedy can be effected without delay. But if no spare spring is available, nor a spare reel, the fisherman will have no alternative except to carry on fishing with a free running reel. This is not so impossible as it sounds, although risky. The trouble will not start until a fish is hooked; then he will have to use his fingers as a brake when the fish takes out line. He may get the tips of them burnt! and would be well advised to put on a glove if he has one. But if the fish is not too wild and strong, it is possible he may be able to control it sufficiently to stop the reel over-running and jamming. If he is playing the fish from a boat, he can pull off a lot of line from the reel and let it fall on the bottom of the boat, simply playing the fish by holding the line and letting it go when the pressure becomes too great, and pulling line in again when the fish stops running; but with loose line lying about there is always the risk of it becoming hitched up round some obstruction, so this should be attempted with caution.

Another difficulty occurs with reels, if the handle comes off and cannot be fixed on again. This is not necessarily too serious a calamity if some substitute for the handle can be found—two or three matchsticks wedged in the aperture or something like a small pencil, trimmed short, or even a suitably sized screw jammed into it can save the situation to the extent of making it possible to wind in line on the drum if a fish is being played. It may not be comfortable but it may just be good enough to save the situation. The only other alternative is to take in line by hand as described above. This is not too impossible, provided the angler keeps cool and collected. It is much easier if the tackle is strong and as the fish tires.

Landing nets should always be carefully watched so that no holes which form in them go unspotted. It is so easy to tear a net on such obstructions as barbed wire or sharp branch ends. Any hole once made, even a small one, is liable quickly to increase in size to a point where a fish can slip through it. It is a simple repair to tie up such a hole with some braided nylon or string, or even with nylon monofilament if nothing else is available, and this should never be neglected.

Split-cane rods often have metal ferrule joints and fibre glass and carbon graphite rods spigot joints. Such joints, if left unbroken for a length of time, have a nasty habit of becoming jammed and immovable by a single person. Two people, however, can usually loosen them by combined effort. The best way is for one individual to grasp the rod with one hand *below* the joint, and the other hand *above* it. The second individual does the same. They then twist in the appropriate directions. This usually succeeds, but if not the help of a third individual should be enlisted to increase the twisting pressure. I have never known this to fail. In the case of metal ferrules jammed fast, a series of matches, or better a candle, can be used to apply heat to the female ferrule. This method, too, seldom seems to fail; but it dirties the ferrule, and care must be taken not to let the flame approach anywhere near the wood. It should only be employed as a last resort.

When one is walking through bushes or woods or

climbing fences it is easy to spring a rod ring from its seating, if one's rod gets hung up. A turn or two of the sticky tape described above will effect an immediate temporary repair, which again should not be neglected. The ring can be properly re-whipped into position later. Another tiresomeness is if an agate top-ring becomes cracked from contact with a stone or some other hard object. It should always be replaced at once, or lasting damage may be done to the line dressing—steel rings in contrast do not crack but they groove badly with continued use. They too should be changed when necessary. Ice forming in rod rings on a cold spring or autumn day is another possible hazard, which can be a serious annoyance. Greasing the rings thickly with vaseline may help to prevent this; but there is another method for the fly fisherman—having put out a reasonable length of line, he should carry on fishing with the same length of line, neither shortening or lengthening it, and without any shooting. Thus little or no water will be deposited on the rings (anyhow until a fish is hooked), and ice will take a long time to form on them if it does so at all.

Gaff points and hook points should be kept keenly sharp at all times, as well as rust-free. A small piece of carborundum stone in the pocket, or a flat stone from the river bed should be used to ensure this, and the gaff point should be greased from time to time.

If a salmon in the course of play becomes snagged round a stone in the river bed, quick action is necessary or he will soon get rid of the hook or break the leader. Wading out as far as possible into mid-river well downstream or upstream of the snag may enable the angler to clear the line; or if a boat is available it is a simple matter to row over towards the far bank and free the line from downstream (or from upstream if the fish has travelled in a downstream direction). Failing this there may perhaps be time for the fisherman to put his rod down and construct a quick extempore 'otter' from a long and pliable withy shoot, if one happens to be growing nearby, twisted into a circle and passed over the rod butt, and so down the line. If worked from well upstream as far down the line as possible, such an 'otter' will sometimes free the line, and with luck the salmon may still be found on the end. If already played for a fair time, and tired as a result, fish will usually lie quiet for several minutes when they are snagged. If still full of energy, however, they will quickly break free, as is only to be expected.

A pair of brogues which are too tight, especially when worn with thick wading socks, are another unpleasant liability. If worn for any length of time, apart from being disagreeably uncomfortable they may do physical damage to the feet. Pressure can often be eased by splitting the upper cover of the toe in one or more places with the aid of a sharp knife, or by slitting elsewhere in the leather or rubber, as needed. Brogues do not need to be waterproof, so provided the cutting is carried out with discretion no damage need be done. One other contingency needs to be considered, and that is the unfortunate one of a hook becoming embedded beyond the barb in some person's anatomy. Once the barb is well covered no time should be wasted in painful and almost certainly futile efforts at abstraction. Recourse should at once be had to the local doctor, who if he lives near a prolific salmon river will probably be well used to such mishaps. A local anaesthetic and some deft work with a scalpel will quickly put an end to the trouble, and fishing can be resumed without further loss of time.

17
Hooks

Of the salmon that we pull and hook, what proportion do we actually bring to the bank without their becoming unhooked? It is worth taking note of this, and if the proportion seems to be too low it could to some extent be due to bad handling on our part during play; but surely it is just as likely to be due to our using indifferent hooks? Careful thought about hooks in general, and determination to use only those of first rate quality, could quite possibly lead to a substantial reduction in losses.

The hook is the first link between the angler and his prey, and perhaps the most important. It is essential that it should be well-tempered to the right extent, not too softly so that it straightens out, nor too hard so that it becomes brittle. In this respect hand forged hooks are better than mass produced ones, though it may be hard to obtain them. There is much more margin for error in hooks tempered in large numbers together, and individual defects are more difficult to spot. If you are a fly tyer always have a good look at your hook before you put in some elaborate tying on it. You may have wasted a lot of time and effort if you find subsequently that it lacks a barb or point.

A second essential desirability in a hook is that the point should always be penetratingly sharp, and should at all times be kept so. A sliver of carborundum stone carried in the pocket will help to achieve this, or failing that a small piece of flat stone picked up from the river-bed will be nearly as good. Even a pen-knife blade, used as for sharpening a pencil, can help. The author was once shown some hooks specially made for the great Wye fisherman, Mr Robert Pashley. They were fine and sharp to a degree, and such hooks without doubt must have secured many a good fish for him, which on blunter or coarser patterns would have come unstuck. Bluntness in a hook point must give rise to many an abortive pull, or to the hook not penetrating beyond the barb, so that the fish rids himself of it after a minute or two's play.

While on the subject of barbs, it is of course essential for a sound hook hold that the point should at once become buried beyond the barb in the fish's flesh. Only then is the hook likely to remain fast. One remembers in one's young days trying to use big single-hooked flies of sizes 4/0 to 6/0 on a rod of 13 feet or 14 feet and how many fish came unhooked on such tackle, simply because one did not hold them hard enough when they took (or more probably *couldn't* do so with such a light rod), so that the big hook never got buried beyond the barb. It needs great pressure to get big hooks of this size thus well buried, but once they are they take a tremendous hold. A rod of 16 feet or longer is needed to fish them effectively, and to ensure that they become well buried in the fish's mouth.

There is also, in any hook, some significance in the position of the barb. One would have thought that the nearer the point the less pressure would have to be exerted for the barb to be engaged; and some brands of hooks do have their barbs very close to the point. In my view this is an advantage, and I would eschew hooks that have a long point before the barb is reached.

In the tackle catalogues of seventy years ago one sees that hooks were on sale with two barbs near the point, one on each side. This would have seemed a good idea, though it dropped out of fashion. Perhaps our present day hook makers would consider resurrecting such a pattern?

Thickness of metal in the hook is another factor which should be taken into consideration. The stouter the metal, the stronger the hook, it is true; but penetration must become ever more difficult as the hook becomes thicker and clumsier. Also it is difficult to fashion a really sharp point on the thicker metal. Fine wire on the other hand leads to easier penetration, but is more likely to bend or break under strain. It is also more likely to tear through the hook-hold. So a happy medium is called for in thickness of metal, governed to a considerable extent by such relevant considerations as size of fish expected, strength of current, and width of river, for instance one would need a very different strength of metal fishing for grilse in a small west coast river than for forty pounders in the Sundal or Evanger.

Whether to use single, double or treble hooks depends on the circumstances. Personally I have largely given up using single hooks on the grounds that doubles or trebles take a better hold. I do use singles however for dropper flies, as I find they are less likely to become caught up, and prefer a short shanked round or snecked bend. I do not like the long shanked fine wire single hooks advocated by Mr A. H. E. Wood of Cairnton, as these seem far too liable to pull out during play.

As to double hooks, for years I used these with confidence up to about size 4, though no larger. They seemed to take a better hold than singles, and one lost fewer fish with them. They are useful as an alternative to singles for droppers. Possibly one gets marginally more tangles when using them, particularly on a long line, but not seriously so. I am never afraid to use them for this purpose. They are better than singles if one wants to use very small flies of size 10 or smaller, but nevertheless seldom take a good hold in such diminutive proportions, and one loses many of the fish that are hooked on them.

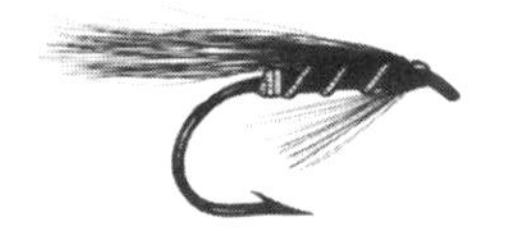

A short-shanked good dropper fly

Treble hooks have recently come into general popularity, either for flies tied on their shank, or for use with tube flies of any size from minute to four inches in length. There is a great deal to be said for them. In any size they seem to hook and hold better than either doubles or singles, provided they are of the type that possesses the desirable qualities listed above. It takes slightly more pressure in the first place for them to be driven well home in the fish's mouth than either a double or single, but not enough to constitute a drawback. For really big flies of three to four inches long they are an acceptable alternative in appropriate size to the big single hook, and lose fewer fish. For fishing in Norway for big fish, in outstandingly strong rivers, the big single hook works fairly well, but a proportionately smaller treble of sound metal is as good. Fine wire trebles are particularly good for normal fly fishing; they seem to hook and hold well. In very small sizes for grilse or summer salmon they are probably the best type of hook mount for a fly, better than either doubles or singles; though in the case of grilse one still seems to lose a disproportionately large number of the fish one hooks. These fish have very soft mouths and are very active in play, jumping, twisting and turning to an exasperating extent. There seems to be no tackle yet invented (other than the despicable worming outfit!) which will hold a fair majority of them, and hooks of whatever type are by no means entirely to blame.

In spite of their many advantages treble hooks are not the final answer. When fish are taking badly, they pull at them without being hooked, or get rid of them in play time and time again. It can be maddening, and one is apt to wonder how on earth they manage it. But as pointed out elsewhere in this book fish must be lost from time to time, otherwise there would be no fun at all in playing them, and in addition the stocks would be sadly reduced. On these difficult occasions, it must also be remembered that if treble hooks perform badly, doubles or singles would doubtless be worse. Treble hooks mounted on plugs and spoons are particularly liable to come away. It is not surprising when they are masked in their hooking action by such a substantial bait.

For bait fishing of all descriptions the treble hook is the dominant pattern, and rightly so. But care should be taken that the metal is not too fine, when baits are frequently snagged on the river bed. In any form of bait fishing, other than with very light tackle, becoming snagged seems a common occurrence, and hooks can be easily strained in the freeing process. Therefore they should be strong, and fine wire hooks are of little use for this purpose.

In every case, whether single, double or treble, when a hook has become bent in any direction or opened out, it should be ruthlessly discarded. How great is the temptation simply to bend it back into proper shape, and continue fishing with it, we all know! It saves so much time and trouble, and allows us to get on with the job without further delay. To do this is a bad mistake; the metal has first been weakened by the original bend and is weakened again by the return bend. If it subsequently breaks and causes the loss of a fish, the angler has only himself to blame. A treble in particular, when it has one of its hooks opened out, even to a small extent, should not be used any further. That particular hook has been weakened, and it is the one of the three which, owing to its outurned angle, is most likely to take hold in the fish's mouth.

Much attention is devoted to the eyes of hooks and whether they should be upeyed or downeyed. The upeyed hook appears neater and for that reason is to be recommended, though really there can be little practical difference between the two types. One small point to be looked for about the eye of the hook is that it should bulge outwards to some little extent, so that a turn or two of the leader round its base can grip fast in a knot, and not slip off at the top.

Rust is a harmful factor which should never be allowed to obtain a hold on hooks. If substantially developed it can weaken the metal, destroy the barb, and blunt the point; and a hook so afflicted should be jettisoned. A slight coating of rust can be scraped off with a pen-knife, and prevented from recurring by grease or oil.

Hooks can be cracked or broken, particularly by overhead casters, on stones or rocks behind. If you watch an overhead caster performing, particularly if he is trying to throw a long line, you will sometimes hear a sharp crack as his fly on the back cast hits an obstruction behind. The caster himself may well not have heard it, and be unaware that anything is wrong. The hook however in such a case will be almost certainly damaged, either by loss of its point(s) so that it cannot hold a fish, or else through being cracked, so that it will break in the next fish that takes it. Often in the latter case the angler blames the hook for being unsound, which is untrue and unfair. As to various patterns of hook we find a variety of examples. 'Outpoints' are still made, the idea being that a hook so fashioned is more likely to take a hold than one with its point turned inwards or in strict parallel with the shank. The idea is readily understandable and perhaps commendable; though the angle of pull when a fish has taken would be more direct with the hook point in line with the shank or even turned slightly inwards. In actual use however outpoints seem reliable, and I would not hesitate to use one if it was made of sound metal. Quadruple hooks have been produced, out-rivalling treble hooks in so-called hooking capacity. In fact they would seem to hold no advantage over trebles, and are bulkier and more clumsy. They are not to be recommended. The question of leverage is also one of some moment. The longer the shank and the narrower the gape of the hook, the greater obviously will be the leverage on the hook-hold, when a fish is being played and pressure applied from various different directions as he turns and twists. The greater the leverage the more likely the hook is to tear out. The old fashioned 'Dee' fly hooks were notorious offenders in this respect, with their ultra long shank and narrow gape. It is hard in any case to see the need for a long shank. It may give greater scope for a skilled fly-tyer to adorn his creation with an elaborate jointed and hackled body, but we now know this to be unnecessary in order to attract salmon, whatever the Victorian fishermen may have thought. Giving weight to the fly, so that it would sink deeper if required, was another possible consideration. But nowadays we can achieve this more easily through sinking lines or metal tubes, so that a long and consequently heavier shank is unnecessary. Indeed from the advantageous point of view of avoiding leverage, one would say that the shorter the shank in any type of hook the better.

Snecked bend single hooks, with a short shank, as mentioned above, are good for droppers. They take a firm hold.

Esmond Drury hooks, treble fly-hooks with a longer shank than normal, are first rate. The extra length of shank is not enough to exert undue leverage, and it facilitates the dressing of the fly.

Patterns of treble-hooked flies

Fine wire trebles, with their merits and drawbacks, have already been mentioned. There is a particularly good French brand of such trebles.

There have been many other different and peculiar types of hook which have been produced in the past, . . .

one for instance had a hinged joint half way down the shank, with the object of reducing leverage. But they have not stood the test of time and service, and have for the most part disappeared.

Finally, there is the all-important principle of relating the size of the hook to that of the fish expected and the size of the lure. 'Big hooks for big fish and small hooks for small fish' broadly speaking is the right axiom. For fish of thirty to fifty pounds, for example, in a strong Norwegian river, it is quite useless using flies of size 4 or smaller. If fish take them it is forty to one that such a small hook in due course will simply tear out. 4/0 hooks or bigger, or treble hooks, larger than normal, are what are needed. They alone will obtain a secure enough hold to stand up to the violent stress involved. Turning to the opposite extreme, if one wants to catch grilse with an occasional summer salmon in Scotland in July, somewhere where the grilse far outnumber the salmon, one needs small hooks of fine wire with very sharp points. Big hooks are much too clumsy for the soft mouths and active play of grilse, as we all know. They would produce little except pulls and losses, if the fish did not fight shy of them altogether.

In the intermediate stages this principle holds good, except that in spring or autumn when cold water necessitates the use of a large sized lure the size of hooks should be increased proportionately. It is useless for example fishing tiny trebles on a large sized spoon or golden sprat, as I have seen done, and then being surprised when a hooked salmon goes on his way rejoicing. Always the size of the hook should be kept in proportion firstly to the size of the fish and secondly, it must be added, to the size of the lure.

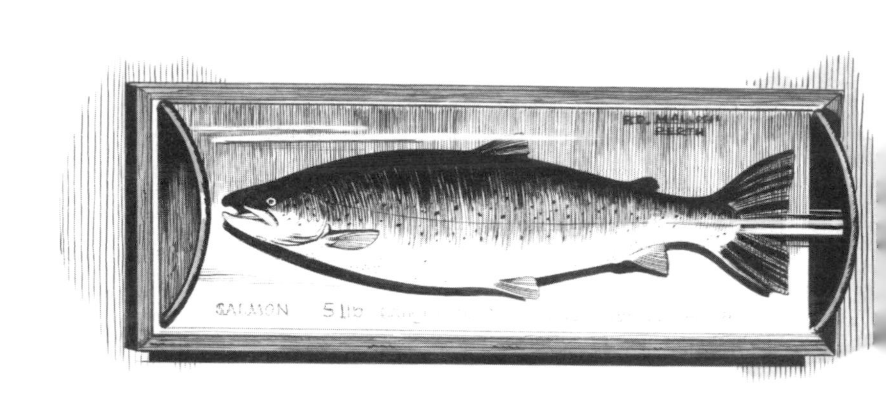
PERTH
SALMON 5 lb

IV

SHOOTING A LINE

18

Big Fish From British Rivers

There is a fascination about big fish whether caught or lost on rod and line. Fifty pounds seems a good criterion for those caught and listed (forty pounders are too numerous) and salmon of this weight are beyond the wildest hopes of the vast majority of British anglers.

Here is a record of most of the fifty pounders or over which have been caught in Britain on fly. It is doubtless incomplete, but so far as it goes it is accurate. Here too are records of the capture of many other fish of this weight, where the lure they took is not stated, but in some cases it is likely to have been a fly. I have also made a list of the six largest fifty pounders or over killed for certain on bait.

The listing, even if not complete, is perhaps longer than might have been expected, fifty or even forty pounders being so scarce in these present days. The reason for this scarcity is obvious. Too many fish are now killed in the sea by drift net and long line before they ever have a chance to grow to this size (which normally entails a sea life over three or more consecutive winters), and before they return to fresh water to breed. Lists like these therefore make melancholy reading, in that they relate to dates so long past. (The last fish in the fifty pound category that I remember hearing about was caught at Ballathie on the Tay some eighteen years ago.) But at least they should be kept in mind if only to show what we are lacking in present days as regards size of fish. The Wye, Spey, and Tay nowadays probably offer the best chance of all British rivers for a really big fish, but no doubt many Norwegian rivers provide much better prospects in this field.

FIFTY POUNDERS AND OVER CAUGHT IN BRITAIN ON FLY

61lb Caught by Mrs Morrison in the Wood o'Shaws pool, Mountblairey Water, River Deveron, on October 21st 1924. This fish took a $1\frac{1}{4}$ inch fly. It was not weighed till 24 hours after capture, so its original weight may have been heavier. It measured 53 ins by 33 ins, and is the largest fish ever caught on fly so far in Britain.

60lb Caught by Mr Lowther Bridger in 1888 on the Cumberland Eden. This fish measured 54 ins by 27 ins. It is the largest fish ever caught on fly in England.

$57\frac{1}{2}$lb Caught by Mr Pryor on the Floors Castle water, River Tweed, on October 27th 1886. The fly was a Silver Wilkinson 4/0. This fish again was not weighed until the morning after its capture, so may originally have been heavier. Mr Pryor caught 15 fish altogether that day.

57lb Caught by Michael Maher, a ghillie, on the Longfield water, River Suir, in the spring of 1874. This is the record rod-caught salmon for Ireland. The fly was a home-made one, subsequently christened the 'Mystery'. There is a detailed account of the capture of this fish in Sir Herbert Maxwell's *Fishing at Home and Abroad*.

57lb Caught by Major A. W. Huntington in the Cassan Dhu pool, River Awe, on July 8th 1921. This fish measured 52½ ins by 27½ ins and was caught on a Mar Lodge 3/0. Major Huntington caught a second fish of 51lb in the River Awe (see below).

57lb Caught on the Syndicate water, River Awe, on October 8th 1909, the fly being the only lure allowed on this water. This fish is recorded by Augustus Grimble on page 96 of the third edition of his *Salmon and Trout Rivers of Scotland*, but the name of the captor is not mentioned.

56lb Caught by Col. A. E. Scott on the Deveron on October 31st 1920. The fly was a 1/0 Britannia. This fish measured 50 ins by 29 ins.

56lb Caught by Mr H. G. Thornton in Pol Verie on the River Awe on June 12th 1923. This fish took a 5/0 fly. It was hooked at 1 p.m. and landed at 3.30 p.m.

55½lb Caught by Mr P. M. Coats at Stobhall on the Tay in October 1903. The fly was a Wilkinson

55lb Caught by the Marquess of Zetland in the Mill Stream at Stobhall, River Tay, in October 1895. This fish measured 50 ins by 30 ins and took a Claret Major.

55lb Caught by Mr W. A. Kidson in the River Tweed in November 1913. (The fly is the only lure allowed on the Tweed in autumn.)

55lb Caught by Mr Brereton at Mertoun on the River Tweed in the autumn of 1889. The fly was 'a small Wilkinson'.

54lb Caught by Lord Ruthven in the Findford pool at Stobhall on the River Tay on October 4th 1883. The fly was a No. 2 Jock Scott.

53lb Caught by Mr O. M. Pritchard on the Lower Scone water, River Tay, on October 15th 1924. This fish measured 51¼ ins by 29 ins.

53lb Caught by Lord Blythswood in the Sandy Ford pool, Stobhall water, River Tay, in the autumn of 1899. This fish took 'a medium sized Black Dog'. The Sandy Ford pool is now on the Islamouth beat.

53lb Caught by A. McColl (ghillie) in the Disputed Pool, River Awe, in 1913. The fly was a Childers.

53lb Caught by Mr W. G. Craven in the Dallachy Pool, Gordon Castle Water, River Spey, in the autumn of 1897. This is the record Spey rod-caught fish, and it took a No. 4 Carron Fly. It was landed in a quarter of an hour.

53lb Caught by Sir Stuart Coats at Cargill on the River Tay on October 15th 1923. This fish measured 49 ins by 29 ins and took a Jock Scott.

52lb Caught by Mr L. Ferguson on the Cumberland Derwent in 1885. This fish is recorded in Jock Scott's *Game Fish Records* as being caught on fly.

51½lb Caught by Gen. Home at Birgham Dub on the River Tweed in the autumn of 1902. This fish took a Jock Scott.

51½lb Caught by Mr J. Gellatly at Ballathie, River Tay, in July 1875. This fish was caught on a sea-trout fly.

51½lb Caught by Dr Fison at Norham on the Tweed in October 1922. This fish measured 50¾ ins by 27 ins.

51lb Caught by Sir Stuart Coats at Ballathie on the River Tay on October 7th 1913, on fly.

51lb Caught by Dr C. Child near Taynuilt on the River Awe in September 1907 on a 'Blue Doctor'.

51lb Caught by Mr A. Lees-Milne on the Awe in October 1913.

51lb Caught by Mr Howard St George on the Tweed on February 11th 1921. This fish took a Jock Scott, and was most probably a late run autumn fish. It measured 54 ins by 24½ ins.

51lb Caught by Major A. W. Huntington on the Awe on May 22nd 1930. This fish was hooked in the Stepping Stones and took a 5/0 Green Highlander.

50½lb Caught by Dr J. Rudd at Birgham Dub on the River Tweed in the autumn of 1925.

50½lb Caught by Mr P. Loudoun in the Black Pool below Mount Annan, River Annan. The fly was a Brown Turkey.

50lb Caught by Lord Winterton in the Rock Pool, Gordon Castle water, River Spey, in the autumn of 1880.

50lb Caught by A. Fraser (ghillie) in the Falls Pool, River Beauly, in October 1909.

50lb Caught by Miss Lettice Ward at Kinnaird on the River Tay on October 12th 1928. This fish measured 51¾ ins by 27½ ins.

50lb Caught by Colonel H. Clarke-Jervoise in Finford Head at Stobhall on the River Tay on September 23rd 1883. This fish took a 2/0 Jock Scott.

FIFTY-THREE POUNDERS OR OVER CAUGHT IN BRITAIN ON BAIT

The seven biggest British salmon caught on bait were as follows:

64lb Caught by Miss Georgina Ballantine in the Boat Pool on the Glendelvine water, River Tay, on October 7th 1922. This is the biggest British rod-caught salmon. It was caught harling, and took a spinning bait described as a 'dace', and whether this bait was artificial or natural is now open to question. Miss Ballantine unfortunately died a few years ago. This fish was played for two hours and landed below Caputh bridge.

61½lb Caught by Mr T. Stewart on the last day of the season 1907 on the River Tay below Perth. This fish was caught on worm.

61lb Caught by Mr J. Haggart on the River Tay in 1870.

59½lb Caught by Miss Doreen Davy at Lower Winforton on the River Wye on March 12th 1923. This fish took a devon minnow. It is the record British spring fish.

58lb Reported from the River Shannon in 1872, but possibly not caught by fair angling, as the 57lb Suir fish (see p. 217) is regarded as the record Irish rod-caught fish.

55lb Caught by Mrs Huntington on the River Awe on September 19th 1927. This fish was hooked in Errochd pool and landed in Dalraede.

53lb Caught by Mr Dow on the River Tay below Perth in 1915.

Here also is a list of a number of other fifty pounders killed in Britain, but whether on fly or bait is not certain:

59lb Caught by Mr Somerville on the South Esk at Kinnaird, in October 1888.

56lb Caught by J. Gordon (ghillie) on the Ardoe water on the Aberdeenshire Dee in October 1888.

56lb Caught by G. Mackenzie (gamekeeper) at Warwick Hall on the River Eden in November 1892.

55½lb Caught by Mr E. Francis at Corby on the Eden in 1888.

55½lb Caught by Capt. A. G. Goodwin on the Tay on September 28th 1898. This fish measured 50 ins by 30 ins.

54lb Caught by Sir J. B. Lawes on the River Awe in 1877.

54lb Caught by the schoolmaster of Taynuilt on the River Awe in 1880 (?). This fish was hooked in Cassan Dhu and landed at Crubeg.

54lb Caught by Mr F. Milburn at Doonas on the Shannon in 1903.

53lb Caught by Mr W. Ivis on the Shannon in 1914.

52lb Caught by Mr A. Macbeth at Kinnaird on the River Tay in 1917.

52lb Caught by Mr M. Ewen at Park on the Dee in October 1918.

52lb Caught by Dr J. P. McGowan on the Don in October 1924.

51lb Caught by Mr E. Fieldhouse on the Tay in 1905.

51lb Caught by Mr P. M. Coats on the Tay in 1903.

50lb Caught on the Annan in November 1919.

The biggest authenticated British salmon of modern times weighed 84lb and was caught in 1869 in a net low down in the Firth of Tay by one, Wullie Walker. It was said that he could talk of little else for the rest of his lifetime!

19

Tall But True

Anything *can* happen fishing. Most fishermen have their quota of tall stories which they like to narrate. Here are a few of the author's, every one of them meticulously true.

Kelts in Summer

I have seen a kelt caught on a fly in the month of July. This happened in 1980 in the Kelt Pool on the Grimersta. This wretched fish must have been isolated by continual low water after spawning in some remote corner, and up till July it had never succeeded in reaching the sea. A second kelt was caught on the Grimersta later the same week. One wonders how on earth these fish managed to survive for so long.

I have also seen a kelt caught in early August. This was at Delfur on the Spey in the 1950s. It was a black hen fish, very thin, which had shed all its spawn. Such a fish could not be classed as anything but a kelt; although there had been nothing to stop it returning to the sea at any time. It appeared to have spawned quite recently.

I have also seen a kelt caught on the Lochy in September. The captor did not realise his misfortune, and as he was so pleased with his capture I did not disillusion him. This again was a black hen fish which had lost all its spawn—presumably a very early spawner.

A Kelt with Sea Lice

In April 1953 I was fishing Carnegie, a pool on the Rothes beat of the Spey which lies at about 14 miles above tidal water. There were still plenty of kelts about, and presently I caught one. It was bright silver but very thin, even for a kelt. There was nothing unusual about this; but just before returning it to the river I noticed to my astonishment a number of large female sea-lice attached to it in the usual places. This enterprising fish had evidently dropped back to the sea, and entered the river again in company with some fresh salmon. It was certainly surprising to find it so far up-river.

Twice a salmon has been landed with both tail and dropper flies hooked in its mouth

Fishing on the Spey in summer I often used to use two flies, tail and dropper in fairly small sizes. On two different occasions at Delfur I landed a salmon, and found both flies firmly hooked in its mouth.

Obviously these fish had first taken the tail fly and then swum on to take the dropper too. The strain in play would have been taken by the dropper attachment while the pressure of the current on the lower part of the leader must have set the tail fly hook in the fish's mouth. There is no other possible explanation.

Eight salmon in eight consecutive casts

Fishing at Teviot mouth in the Junction Pool at Kelso on the Tweed on February 15th 1956 I caught 8 salmon in 8 consecutive casts. (Admittedly the last of these fish was a kelt.) All these were on a golden sprat. There was no special skill of any sort attached to this performance, in fact it could hardly have been easier, though it seemed miraculous on one's first day's fishing that season. The noteworthy aspect of it lies in showing the prolific stock of spring fish that at this period were to be found in the Tweed.

A flounder hooked in the mouth

Fishing in the Cabin at Careysville on the Cork Blackwater in the 1950s I felt a curious sort of drag at the end of my line, rather like a lump of weed, and yet it kicked. I was using a three inch golden sprat at the time, and when I reeled in I found a small flounder or dab of about nine inches in length had taken it and was hooked *in the mouth.* A somewhat unexpected anticlimax, but one has to take what comes up!

A salmon caught by handlining

Fishing at Careysville in March 1962, I was standing on the lower level of the Quay Wall, and casting a largish fly into the pool of that name. I had completed my forward throw but suspected that the fly was not fishing correctly. Instead of fishing out the cast I therefore put my rod under my elbow, caught hold of the dressed line a yard or two below the rod point, and started to haul in the line, cast, and fly fairly quickly, hand over hand. I had pulled in perhaps five yards of line when I suddenly felt a fish take. I did the only thing I could which was to strike and play him for perhaps half a minute by hand. When I felt that with any luck he was firmly enough hooked I dropped the line and took up the slack with the rod point. He was still there, and I landed him, well hooked. He weighed 14lb.

A hooked fish jumps onto the bank

My friend the late Col. J. P. Moreton was playing a fish in a pool called Haddon's Hole on the Cork Blackwater at Careysville. The left side of this pool has a sheer drop of perhaps 4 feet down into deep water right under the bank. This fish, after being played a short time, came in close to the side, and then unexpectedly did a violent jump right out of the water onto the high bank above. Ghillie Maloney fell upon it with delight! and roaring with laughter.

Off and on

On more than one occasion in the 1950s, when playing a fish in the Flats at Careysville, my quarry came unhooked in mid-river; but this was not the end of it. As I regretfully reeled my minnow back towards the bank a second fish took it and was successfully landed. One hardly noticed the loss! This is perhaps nothing particularly noteworthy about this, except that it happened more than once and bid fair to show the extent of the salmon stocks which often lay in the Careysville water at that time.

A fish on the back throw of the Spey cast

My daughter was fishing a pool called Landslide on the Vatnsdalsa in north Iceland. There was little current in this pool, which was really the outlet from a lake. She was Spey casting quite proficiently, but after several casts the line refused to go out, unexpectedly, on the forward throw. It took a few seconds to realise what had happened. A salmon had in fact taken the fly as it pitched into the water close to her feet on the retrieve from the previous cast. This fish was well hooked and was successfully landed.

No leader

One of my friends, acting as boatman for his son on the Tweed one autumn, as an experiment attached the fly directly to the dressed line, omitting to use any monofilament. It was taken quite quickly by an enterprising salmon which was firmly hooked and subsequently landed.

An arctic tern on the fly

In Iceland the arctic terns were very bold. As long as their young were unfledged they used to make repeated dive-bombing attacks on anyone in the neighbourhood. They also used to hover over one's fly as it fished round, and would dive down attempting to catch it. One day one of them did succeed in catching my fly, as I did not pull it away from him quickly enough, and he was hooked. He played rather like a kite! I did not want to hurt him if I could possibly help it, so I handlined him gently, gradually shortening the line. Every now and then he would lose balance and volplane down into the water, again like a kite, only to labour up aloft once more, though on a shortened line. Eventually I was able to catch hold of him. He did not help, but pecked aggressively. Fortunately he was only lightly hooked through the beak.

I was able to disengage the hook without doing him harm, and feeling rather like Noah with his dove I quietly opened my hands and launched him forth. He flew off, none the worse, but with loud squawks of indignation.

A record smallest grilse?

One hears a lot about big salmon caught in various countries. But what about the opposite end of the scale? Occasionally one encounters very small grilse. Some of the ones we caught in Iceland were indeed undersized. My own record was $1\frac{1}{2}$lb, a perfectly shaped grilse and definitely not a sea-trout, as many grilse of this small size would have been labelled. It was caught on the Laxa a Asum in company with a number of other grilse from 3–6lb of which there were plenty.

A salmon broken in a pool when being beached, and caught three days later in the same pool with the original fly still in its mouth

Occurrences of this sort are apparently not altogether rare, and I have more than once caught fish with fly or bait hooks fast in their mouth, and seen others catch fish so afflicted.

The following event may perhaps be of interest. In the Green Banks pool of the Vatnsdalsa in north Iceland a friend of mine some years ago was about to beach a salmon of 12lb which he had hooked and played. At the last moment the nylon leader broke, and the fish, although played out, made off with the fly still in his mouth. Three days later another friend was fishing the same pool, and hooked a fish which I, as ghillie, netted for him. I was kneeling on the bank to extract the fly from the fish's mouth, having hit it on the head, and I recognised the fly as one of my own tying. Having freed the fly I suddenly realized it was not attached to my friend's leader, and it was in fact the fly which I had given to my first friend and on which this fish had been lost three days before. The second fly was still fast in the fish's mouth but was not so obvious. The fish had definitely taken both flies, as both hooks were buried in the flesh, and it was not that the second fly had fouled the loose nylon attached to the first fly.

It was surely unusual for a fish to have taken again so soon after being played right out on the first occasion, and to have stayed in the same pool throughout? I witnessed both episodes, acting as ghillie.

Salmon in succession hooked and lost

There is a story of a Spey fisherman casting from a ledge on the rock face at Craigellachie bridge on the Spey, who hooked 19 grilse in one morning long ago, and lost 18 of them! Whether this is true or not I would not like to say, but I know I have myself hooked and lost nine fish running on one occasion in Iceland—a depressing experience without any ostensible cause. It made one wonder at the time whether or not it was worth while continuing to fish!

On two different occasions a fish is hooked on a devon minnow mounted on an Alasticum wire trace, but after the fish has been landed the devon has disappeared

This sounds a very 'tall' story, but in both cases it did, almost inexplicably, occur. I was fishing at Rothes on the Spey in the 1950s when I landed these two fish on a devon minnow on two different occasions, and suddenly to my amazement noticed that in both cases, although the treble hook was fast in the fish's mouth, the devon was nowhere to be seen. Closer investigation showed that the wire trace was inextricably snarled up near its end where it was attached to the swivel on the minnow mount. The join was quite strong and had no doubt been under pressure for some time while the fish were being played. Somehow during play the trace must have looped with the minnow on the loop, then broken so that the minnow dropped off, and the two loose ends of wire pulled together to become firmly intertwined. There can be no other explanation. The join in the wire was small and at first sight hardly apparent. I wonder if any of my readers have ever had a similar experience?

Rolling salmon

Have you ever caught a fish that attempted to escape by rolling? I have, twice; both times on the Spey. A normally hooked salmon on two different occasions seemed only to have the single idea of rolling round and round, and winding the cast and line round his body as round a spindle. It was disconcerting, as one realised during the play exactly what was happening. But when the penny dropped, one also realized that by his doing this the fish could not have been more securely held. When he was landed the line and cast had to be unwound from around him six or eight times, until the fly in his mouth was finally reached. One wonders what on earth induced these fish to play in this extraordinary way? I have never known this to happen to any of my friends or acquaintances, though I seem to recollect reading somewhere about its occurrence elsewhere. I wonder if any of my readers have experienced anything like it? Both these fish were firmly hooked in the mouth, and there was no apparent cause of this amazing behaviour.

A swimming cock pheasant, and a sea eagle

Anglers who are ornithologists may be interested to hear the following. One morning in May 1968, when I was fishing on the Spey at Knockando, I had just waded down a long gravelly flat known as Aylmer's Cast, and had turned round to make my way back to the bank. I happened to glance upstream and about 70 yards above me I saw a V in mid-stream formed by some creature swimming across the river from the far side. I wondered idly what it would turn out to be, expecting a water rat or a mink or possibly a squirrel. But to my astonishment the swimmer proved to be a fully grown cock pheasant, which emerged onto the gravel and ran off into the bushes. He had obviously come from the far bank which was high and steep, but why on earth did he adopt this laborious method of crossing the river, which was about 60 yards wide at this point? It seems hard to understand, but unfortunately I never saw the start of his voyage.

On another occasion, when fishing further down the Spey at Rothes, my ghillie James Ross and myself saw a sea-eagle fly up the river from downstream at a height of some 60 feet. This was the biggest bird I have ever seen, having a wing spread of six feet or thereabouts. It appeared two days running, mobbed on both occasions by a swarm of gulls and other birds. On the second day it stooped on a fish in the river, but did not appear to catch it. The only other place where I have seen sea-eagles has been in Iceland where some twenty pairs used to nest each year.

Twice hooked

Major Sir David Wills, a witness of unimpeachable veracity, has contributed an account of the following remarkable episodes:

'I was fishing with a prawn many years ago in Bindon Rush on the river Frome, and my kind host was standing beside me. After two or three casts I said to him: 'The most extraordinary thing has happened; my prawn has just passed me swimming upstream' to which he replied 'But how incredible, it simply can't have!' to which I replied 'But it has!' By that time it had gone out of sight, and a few seconds later a large fish jumped about 30 yards above us. I started to reel in because my line had gone slack, and suddenly found that I was playing a fish. In due course the fish was landed, and when we bent down to take the prawn out of its mouth, lo and behold it was not a prawn that it had in its mouth but a fly! What had happened was that my prawn had picked up a nylon trailer from the fly, wound itself round and round, and was immersed in a complete bird's nest of nylon. It then transpired that the fish, which weighed 29½lb, had been lost by someone fishing on the opposite bank a few days before. This fish, like other lost fish, had been magnified greatly, and our neighbouring fisherman, the doctor who had lost it, had told his friends that he had lost a fish of well over 45lb, which had eventually broken him. My host cut off the tail (with a generous portion), stuck the fly into it, and sent it to the doctor with a little note saying that he thought he would like to have his fly back!

On another occasion I was fishing on the Wye at

Holme Lacey in the 1930s, and in those days I used to use a golden sprat, the mount of which was attached to my line by a wire trace about 2½ feet long. I had hooked a large fish, of over 20lb, just above the Bushes. The fish was very wild and jumped two or three times, but in due course I was able to land it. When I bent down to take the golden sprat out of its mouth, I noticed that the wire trace had broken, but the end of the trace which was still attached to my line had miraculously gone through the eye of the mount, and the wire had then twisted itself over half a turn which was sufficient to keep me attached to my bait and thus to the fish. What must have happened is that when the fish jumped it snapped the trace about 6 inches from the mount, but by a complete fluke the end of the wire, which was springy, went through the eye of the mount and twisted over, all in a split second while the fish was in the air!'

Conclusion

This brings to an end my thoughts about fishing, for the time being. If the reader has persevered thus far with my writing I am greatly in his debt, and would take it as an even higher compliment if he would write to me about anything in it which has aroused his interest, or with which he agrees or does not agree. I hope anyhow that his interest at least at some point or another may have been aroused.

The subject of salmon behaviour coupled with fishing technique is a very wide one, almost unlimited; and it is impossible to cover it adequately in one small volume. One is continuously learning, even after fifty years of fishing, and one's store of knowledge is never anything approaching complete. This year (1983) for instance, in my own case, I hope to delve both in theory and practice into the whole question of dry-fly fishing for salmon, all new to me, and it opens a whole panorama of fresh experiment, an enthralling prospect.

One can never learn how to fish from reading about it. As Alexander Grant, the great Victorian fisherman said, 'Get down to brass tacks' about it, i.e. get down onto the river. The best that books can do is merely to spread new ideas from time to time amongst those who are prepared to devote thought to the subject, and take trouble about it.

Personally I have now reached the stage when not only

the catching of fish (or losing them) is of interest, but even more so seeing others catch them, and acquiring every possible piece of knowledge about salmon and salmon fishing everywhere.

It is a happy goal to have reached, and I wish my readers the best of good fortune on the road towards it, if they have not already arrived there.

Index